An Introduction to the
Psychology of Dreaming

An Introduction to the Psychology of Dreaming

Second Edition

Kelly Bulkeley, PhD

 PRAEGER™

An Imprint of ABC-CLIO, LLC

Santa Barbara, California • Denver, Colorado

Library of Congress Cataloging-in-Publication Data

Names: Bulkeley, Kelly, 1962- author.
Title: An introduction to the psychology of dreaming / Kelly Bulkeley, PhD.
Description: Second edition. | Santa Barbara : Praeger, 2017. | Includes
    bibliographical references and index.
Identifiers: LCCN 2017004678 (print) | LCCN 2017020364 (ebook) |
    ISBN 9781440857072 (ebook) | ISBN 9781440857065 (alk. paper) |
    ISBN 9781440858277 (pbk.)
Subjects: LCSH: Dreams. | Dream interpretation.
Classification: LCC BF1078 (ebook) | LCC BF1078 .B78 2017 (print) |
    DDC 154.6/3—dc23
LC record available at https://lccn.loc.gov/2017004678

ISBN: 978-1-4408-5706-5 (hardcover)
ISBN: 978-1-4408-5827-7 (paperback)
EISBN: 978-1-4408-5707-2

21 20 19 18 17   1 2 3 4 5

This book is also available as an eBook.

Praeger
An Imprint of ABC-CLIO, LLC

ABC-CLIO, LLC
130 Cremona Drive, P.O. Box 1911
Santa Barbara, California 93116-1911
www.abc-clio.com

This book is printed on acid-free paper ∞
Manufactured in the United States of America

For Lightning, Thunder, and Brownie

Contents

Acknowledgments   ix

Chapter 1   Three Basic Questions about Dreaming: Formation,
                 Function, Interpretation   1

Chapter 2   Sigmund Freud Discovers "The Secret of Dreams"   15

Chapter 3   C.G. Jung Descends into the Collective Unconscious   29

Chapter 4   Alternative Clinical Theories about Dreams   43

Chapter 5   Sleep Laboratories, REM Sleep, and Dreaming   59

Chapter 6   Cognitive Psychology and Dreaming   79

Chapter 7   Popular Psychology: Bringing Dreams to the People   101

Chapter 8   Modern Psychology's Answers to the Three Basic
                 Questions about Dreaming   119

*Appendix. The Sleep and Dream Database: A Practical Guide to
Digitally Enhanced Dream Research*   133

Bibliography   143

Index   157

Acknowledgments

I would like to thank Sybe Terwee for introducing me to Greenwood/ ABC-CLIO and encouraging me to take on this project. Doug Daher, George Goethals, Don Browning, Bertram Cohler, and Peter Homans have my deep appreciation for being my most trusted guides in exploring the psychology of dreaming. Of the many dream researchers who have been my teachers and friends over the past several years, five of them—Ernest Hartmann, Johanna King, Carol Schreier Rupprecht, Alan Siegel, and Jeremy Taylor—have given especially valuable support during the original writing of this book. In recent years, I have been fortunate to include more people in this group—G. William Domhoff, Tracey Kahan, Jayne Gackenbach, Patrick McNamara, Ryan Hurd, Anthony Zadra, Deirdre Barrett, Philip King, Bernard Welt, and many others from the International Association for the Study of Dreams. The writings of Anthony Shafton and Robert Van de Castle have provided me with consistently excellent reference materials, and I highly recommend their works. To Chris Altschuler I owe gratitude for regularly providing me with creative inspiration, existential companionship, and fashion tips. To Dr. Polly Young I give thanks for introducing me to *Dientamoeba fragilis*, *Endolimax nana*, and *Blastocystis hominis*, my previously unknown intestinal cohabitants. Rex Marinaro, Joanne Rochon, and Matthew Christianson gave me their expert assistance in the final editing and design of the book, and Debbie Carvalko, Joshua Evans, and Michelle Scott provided support and encouragement in preparing the second edition. And to Hilary, Dylan, Maya, and Conor, thank you for everything.

Three Basic Questions about Dreaming: Formation, Function, Interpretation

I went into a bookstore, like the Cottage Bookstore on 4th Street in San Rafael. There were two people, I think, a man and a woman. The man, the proprietor of the place, offered me some money to kill a man out back. I casually said sure and wrote my name down in some sort of ledger. I went around [to the back of the store] and shot a guy with a gun I had. I wanted $100, but the man told me that I was going to get $25. When I signed my name, I had for some reason given the man a check for $8. Now I started to worry, and it seemed that the man I was dealing with was nervous too. I wanted to get away, but my name in the ledger was evidence of my being there. And I knew the police would question me if I didn't do something. I tried to think of how a purchase plus tax could equal exactly $8. I left going up 4th Street on a bike, I think. It was dusk, and the street was deserted—no people or cars. I was really worried now, thinking first about all the different scenarios in which the police would catch me and then, second, about how readily and nonchalantly I had killed that guy. I hadn't even thought about it before I did it, and now I was shocked at myself.

—Edward, 19-year-old college student

Edward wakes up and says that while he was asleep in his bed he felt like all these things were *really happening* to him; he felt like he was actually experiencing these feelings, activities, and events. He says that certain images and emotions were extremely vivid—the strangely deserted street, the growing fear of the police, the sudden shock of realization that he had killed the man behind the bookstore.

Edward recognizes that many details of the experience are directly related to aspects of his ordinary waking life. The bookstore is a place he has been visiting for years to buy books. Thinking about money, writing checks, and signing his name are all common, daily activities. But other details have no apparent connection to anything in his life. Edward has never been in a major physical fight before, let alone killed anyone. He has never before seen the man and the woman in the bookstore or the man whom he shoots outside. The financial transactions are all very puzzling; Edward feels sure that the $100, $25, and $8 figures mean something, although he does not know what. The whole experience felt very real and somehow terribly meaningful. But Edward is at a loss to say what it was all about.

How do we make sense of such an experience? Is it possible to analyze it, explain it, and understand it?

To begin with, we classify an experience like this as a *dream*. We say that while Edward was asleep in his bed he was dreaming; he dreamed that he went into the bookstore, wrote his name in the ledger, went out and shot the man, and so forth.

But what, then, is a dream?

For thousands of years, humans have been fascinated, intrigued, and perplexed by their dreams. People in cultures all over the world, through all periods of history have wondered about dreaming. Some of the oldest written texts ever discovered are devoted to describing and interpreting people's dreams.

Psychologists have naturally taken a deep interest in dreams. Psychology arose in late 18th-century Europe as an academic discipline devoted to the application of scientific methodologies to the study of the *psyche*—a Greek word that is variously translated as "life," "spirit," "soul," "mind," or "intellect." Dreams, psychologists immediately recognized, are phenomena that offer a means to explore mental structures and processes that are inaccessible to normal waking awareness. By means of careful observation and analysis, psychologists have found that dreams reveal many important aspects of our mental worlds. The dynamics of personality, the workings of perception and memory, the interactions of reason and emotion, the complex relations between mental experiences and bodily functions—these are just some of the important subjects that psychologists have pursued in the study of dreams.

During the 20th and early 21st centuries, the psychological investigation of dreams has expanded tremendously. Using a variety of new methods and techniques, psychologists have studied different types and forms of dreaming, examined the relations of dreaming to other mental processes, and explored the various connections between dreaming and waking. The result of all this research has been nothing less than a revolution in how we view human nature. Anyone who wants to understand the essential qualities of the human mind and its potential for growth must now take into account modern psychological research on dreaming.

This book is an introduction to the major theories of modern psychology regarding dreams and dreaming. It offers a brief history of how these theories have developed from 1900 to the present, along with an extensive bibliography of key books and articles on the contemporary study of dreams. Although the focus is specifically on psychology, some attention will also be given to approaches taken by other fields of study (e.g., anthropology, literature, religion). Attention will also be given to the social, historical, and biographical factors that have shaped this area of research and influenced why psychologists first became interested in dreams, how they have pursued their studies, and what they have discovered.

The major approaches to dreams and dreaming are presented here in a roughly chronological order in order to give readers a sense of how each new approach depends—in complex and varying ways—on those approaches that preceded it. The work of Sigmund Freud is described first, in chapter 2, as he gave the pioneering modern statement on a comprehensive psychology of dreaming. Freud developed an approach to dreams that every subsequent theory has had to acknowledge. The modern psychology of dreaming simply cannot be understood without a solid grounding in Freud's work. Next comes the dream theory of Carl Jung in chapter 3. Although originally a student of Freud, Jung split from him and went on to formulate his own approach to dreams. In many ways, Jung's work has become even more influential than Freud's on modern dream psychology.

Chapter 4 discusses the many alternative clinical views of dreams that have developed out of the therapeutic practices of different psychologists. These approaches offer responses, revisions, and occasionally vigorous challenges to the theories of Freud and Jung. The fifth chapter outlines the body of physiological research generated by the discovery of rapid eye movement (REM) sleep in the 1950s by laboratory researchers at the University of Chicago. This research indicated that the subjective mental experience of dreaming is closely related to complex physiological processes occurring in the brain during sleep. Chapter 6 describes the work

of cognitive psychologists who have used scientifically rigorous methodologies to look at the relationship of dreaming to various processes of
mental functioning (e.g., development of reason, language, memory,
imagination, and cognitive-emotional structures). In chapter 7, the
approaches of popular psychologists are examined. Special attention is
given to their energetic efforts to "democratize" the study of dreams—to
expand the practical applications of psychological theories about dreams
and to make those theories more accessible to the general public.

Many different chronologies of the modern psychology of dreaming
could be constructed, of course. The goal of the particular chronology in
this book is to display as clearly as possible how each new psychological
approach to dreams is related to the approaches that preceded it. If readers learn to recognize these often subtle and complex historical relationships, their understanding of the field as a whole will be greatly enhanced.

Three Basic Questions about Dreaming

Already it should be clear that the modern psychology of dreaming is a
remarkably diverse field of study. Anyone who wants to understand this
field faces the daunting task of trying to make sense of all the different
approaches. The greatest service an introductory book can render is to
help readers in this process. *An Introduction to the Psychology of Dreaming*
will try to give readers an integrated view of modern dream psychology
by focusing its analysis on three basic questions.

The first question is, how are dreams *formed*? Consider Edward's
dream, presented at the beginning of the chapter. How exactly was his
experience created? How was such a vivid, lifelike experiential world
generated in the first place? Given that it occurred while Edward was
sleeping, how was the formation of the dream related to the special mental and physical conditions of being asleep? What role did Edward's cognitive faculties play in forming the dream? At certain points in the dream,
Edward is self-aware, and he rationally reflects on his experiences just as
he might do in waking life. But at other points, seemingly random events
happen to him without his understanding or control. If the dream was
not willed by Edward's waking consciousness, then what did cause it to
happen?

The second basic question is, what *functions* do dreams serve? Is there
a purpose or reason why Edward had this experience? Does his dream
have any adaptive value or evolutionary significance? Does it play some
kind of constructive role in his mental functioning? If so, how could such
values or roles be demonstrated? Are the possible functions of dreams

related in any way to the more general functions of sleep? And what if Edward had not written down his dream when he woke up, but had simply forgotten it—would the experience still serve any important functions? Do dreams have to be consciously remembered and reflected upon to fulfill their functions?

The third basic question is, how can dreams be *interpreted*? Can dreams be understood as expressions of meaning? Does a dream have one fundamental meaning or many different meanings? Or are dreams essentially random nonsense, devoid of any meaning whatsoever? If dreams are assumed to be meaningful, then what kinds of techniques should be used to interpret them? For example, what kind of skills, methods, or special information would be required to interpret Edward's dream? Could Edward interpret his dream himself, or would he need help from someone else? Could someone interpret the dream without knowing anything about Edward? How would we know if an interpretation of his dream was correct? How would we know if an interpretation was not simply reading meanings *into* the dream that are not really there? If two different interpretations are given for the same dream, then can we say that one is better than the other? What criteria would we use to make such a judgment?

Every modern psychological approach to dreaming addresses these three basic questions. The distinct identity of each theory is clearly illustrated by its answers to these three questions. By carefully examining the answers given to these questions by modern psychologists who have studied dreams, readers will be in a good position to evaluate the field as a whole—and then to formulate their own answers.

The Three Basic Questions in Western History

Modern psychologists are not the first to ask about the formation, function, and interpretation of dreams. Many other people throughout history have investigated dreams, reflected on them, developed theoretical models to understand them, and utilized practical methods to apply them in various areas of daily life. A full account of dreams in human history is far beyond the scope of this book. But it is essential for readers to have some awareness of this long and rich history if they want to have a well-grounded understanding of modern dream psychology. Such historical awareness provides a helpful context in which to evaluate the approaches that modern psychologists have taken to the study of dreams and dreaming.

What follows are brief summaries of how dreams are explained and understood in three classic Western sources: the Bible, the philosophy of Aristotle, and the *Oneirocritica* of Artemidorus.

The Bible

The Bible is filled with material on dreams: reports of dream experiences, examples of dream interpretations, and comments on the nature and function of dreams. However, this does not mean that a unified theory of dreams is presented in the Bible. The 66 books that make up the Old and New Testaments were written over the course of many centuries by many different authors with often sharply differing theological views. These books were not collected into a single canonical text until the Vulgate Latin translation by Jerome in the early fifth century CE. It would therefore be foolish to look for a single consistent line of reasoning about dreams across the many books of the Bible. Rather, the Bible offers a variety of perspectives on dreams, and these complex, interrelated perspectives have had a huge influence on Western thought about the experience of dreaming.

The Bible presents dreams as one of the chief means by which God communicates with humans. A primary message conveyed by dreams in the Bible is simply God's immediate, vital presence in the life of the dreamer. This message is illustrated in Abram's experience of "a dread and great darkness" falling upon him (Gen. 15), Jacob's dream of the heavenly ladder (Gen. 28), Samuel's experience in the temple of the Lord (1 Sam. 3), and Solomon's dream at Gibeon (1 Kings 3). Beyond revealing God's numinous presence, many of the dreams also convey messages of reassurance, guidance, and counsel to the dreamers. For example, the book of Matthew describes three dreams experienced by Joseph, the husband of Mary, that reassure him and help him lead his wife and their newborn baby, Jesus, to safety, away from the dangerous King Herod (Matt. 1–2). Similarly, Paul receives dreams that guide him in his missionary work, directing him to be faithful and go preach the gospel in certain needy lands (Acts 16, 18).

A few dreams in the Bible offer specific prophecies of what will happen in the future. Pharaoh's dream of the seven fat cows and seven lean cows, followed by a dream of seven plump ears of grain and seven thin ears of grain, together foretell a coming famine in Egypt (Gen. 41). Gideon overhears a dream described by a Midianite soldier that foretells the victory of Israel over its Midianite enemies (Judg. 7). At times, dreams in the Bible are frightening and serve as warnings to people. Jacob wrestles with a mysterious being until daybreak (Gen. 32), and Job suffers horrible nightmares (Job 7). Abimelech is warned in a dream not to touch Abraham's wife Sarah (Gen. 20), and the Babylonian King Nebuchadnezzar's nightmare warns him that he will be driven mad if he does not submit to God's rule (Dan. 4). While Pontius Pilate sits in judgment of Jesus, his wife says,

"Have nothing to do with that righteous man, for I have suffered much over him today in a dream" (Matt. 27).

The Bible presents two detailed accounts of the practice of dream interpretation. In the first, Joseph interprets the dreams of the baker and the butler (Gen. 40) and of the Pharaoh (Gen. 41). Although Joseph explains in clear, rational terms what the particular images of the dreams mean (e.g., the seven fat and lean cows mean seven years of plentiful harvests followed by seven years of famine), he insists that dream interpretations "belong to God." Joseph says to Pharaoh, "It is not in me; God will give Pharaoh a favorable answer." In the second account, Daniel carefully interprets the dreams of King Nebuchadnezzar (Dan. 1–4). Like Joseph, Daniel explains the symbolic meaning of each image in Nebuchadnezzar's dreams (e.g., a great tree symbolizes the king himself) and says that his interpretive skills are due entirely to God's inspiration and guidance.

A significant aspect of dreams in the Bible is their direct relevance to the broader community. The dreams address the concerns not just of the individual dreamer, but also of the community of God's faithful. When God appears to Solomon in a dream and asks what gift he would like, Solomon says, "Give thy servant therefore an understanding mind to govern thy people, that I may discern between good and evil; for who is able to govern this thy great people?" (1 Kings 3). Likewise, the dreams of Abram, Abimelech, the Midianite soldier, Jacob, Samuel, Joseph, and Paul all express God's care and concern for the welfare of the community.

However, many passages in the Bible also express deep skepticism toward dreams. Dreams are portrayed in Numbers 12 as a potentially deceptive "dark speech," in contrast to the clear revelations of God's presence enjoyed by a prophet like Moses. In the book of Ecclesiastes, it is said, "For a dream comes with much business, and a fool's voice with many words" (Eccl. 5). Similarly, the book of Deuteronomy warns people not to believe those "dreamers of dreams" who promote the idolatrous worship of other gods (Deut. 13). The prophet Jeremiah rails against those who falsely claim to know God's will through their dreams (Jer. 23). There is no naïve, simple-minded acceptance in the Bible of all dreams as divine revelations. While some dreams may indeed disclose God's will, other dreams are dismissed as vain illusions—"on awaking you despise their phantoms" (Ps. 73).

The Philosophy of Aristotle

The Greek philosopher Aristotle (384–322 BCE), a student of Plato's, analyzed dreams in two short treatises, *On Dreams* and *On Prophesying by*

Dreams. Plato had discussed dreams in some of his dialogues, but he never focused on dreams as a particular object of inquiry. Aristotle, however, devotes these two brief works to an examination of dreams, and the views he expresses have had an enduring influence on Western conceptions of dreams (all the more so because his views were essentially restated and endorsed by the Catholic theologian Thomas Aquinas [1224–1275 CE] in his *Summa Theologica*).

In *On Dreams*, Aristotle starts with the observation that when we sleep our faculties of sense perception cease their normal operations; likewise, our intellectual faculties suspend their usual functioning during sleep. So dreams do not arise from sense perceptions or the intellect, which Aristotle believes are the only faculties by which we acquire knowledge. He claims that dreams are caused by echoes of emotionally charged sense perceptions from our daily lives. When we go to sleep, the external objects that we perceive while awake leave the range of our senses; however, there are still impressions from those objects echoing within us, and those echoes themselves become new objects of perception. The problems begin, Aristotle says, when we fail to distinguish those internal echoes from the external objects, and this is precisely what happens in dreams. Aristotle says that dreams are especially liable to mislead us because of the role played by the emotions in them:

> We are easily deceived respecting the operations of sense-perception when we are excited by emotions, and different persons according to their different emotions; for example, the coward when excited by fear, the amorous person by amorous desires; so that, with but little resemblance to go upon, the individual thinks he sees the object of his desire; and the more deeply one is under the influence of the emotion, the less similarity is required to give rise to these illusory impressions. (Aristotle 1941a, 621)

These deceptive, emotionally charged sense impressions make an even greater impact on us when we are asleep, Aristotle argues, because our ordinary powers of reasoning are so diminished. However, he grants that at times our faculties of reason do indeed remain active while dreaming: "For often, when one is asleep, there is something in consciousness which declares that what then presents itself is but a dream" (Aristotle 1941a, 624).

In *On Prophesying by Dreams*, Aristotle evaluates claims that dreams may be divine revelations that foretell the future. He is generally skeptical of such claims because, "it is absurd to combine the idea that the sender of such dreams should be God with the fact that those to whom he sends them are not the best and wisest, but merely commonplace persons" (Aristotle 1941b, 626). Nevertheless, Aristotle says that allegedly prophetic dreams can be regarded in three different ways. They may be causes, tokens, or coincidences (Aristotle 1941b, 626). Dreams may indeed be the cause of future actions, Aristotle argues, for matters of importance in our waking lives regularly appear in our dreams. Just as matters of waking life can influence dreams, "conversely, it must happen that the movements set up first in sleep should also prove to be starting-points of actions to be performed in the daytime" (Aristotle 1941b, 627). He says that dreams may also be tokens of events to come in the future. He refers to dreams that reveal the imminent onset of an illness, before the person has become consciously aware of being sick. Aristotle says that in the quiet of sleep we become aware of slight movements and beginnings that are lost to us in the bustle of daily life: "[I]t is manifest," he says, "that these beginnings must be more evident in sleeping than in waking moments" (Aristotle 1941b, 627).

Having granted all this, Aristotle still believes that "most [so-called prophetic] dreams are, however, to be classified as mere coincidences," especially those that are extravagant or that involve matters with no direct connection to the dreamer. It happens all the time, he argues, that people mistakenly connect two events that are, in fact, unrelated. People make the same error when they connect an unusual dream to an unusual, but actually coincidental, event that comes after the dream.

Regarding the interpretation of dreams, Aristotle's analysis suggests that if we are able to recognize and account for the distorting influence of our emotions, then we may gain genuine and potentially valuable knowledge from our dreams. While dreaming, we sometimes discover in those echoing sense perceptions important features of the world, features that we had overlooked in the busy activities of our waking lives. Aristotle compares dreams to forms reflected in a pool of water: when the water is calm, the forms can be easily perceived; but when the water is troubled (that is, when the mind is agitated by emotion), the reflection becomes distorted and unintelligible. According to Aristotle, the trick to becoming a "skillful interpreter" is learning how to "rapidly discern, and at a glance comprehend, the scattered and distorted fragments of such forms" (Aristotle 1941b, 630). If we can develop this skill, which Aristotle defines as "the faculty of observing resemblances," we may learn something of value from our dreams.

The *Oneirocritica* of Artemidorus

The *Oneirocritica* of Artemidorus of Daldis is by far the longest, most detailed, and most sophisticated text on dreams to survive from ancient times. Artemidorus lived in the second century CE, during a peaceful, prosperous era of the Roman Empire. Few details of his life are known beyond the fact that he was very well read and traveled widely throughout the Mediterranean world. But despite his relative anonymity, Artemidorus has profoundly influenced dream interpreters throughout Western history.

In the *Oneirocritica,* Artemidorus offers a manual for the practical interpretation of dreams. He refers to many other such manuals that he has read, indicating there was a lively tradition of dream literature during this era. Indeed, Artemidorus makes a point of emphasizing that he has studied every book he could find on dream interpretation and that he has even "consorted for many years with the much-despised diviners of the marketplace" (Artemidorus 1975, 13). He goes on to say,

> People who assume a holier-than-thou countenance and who arch their eyebrows in a superior way dismiss them as beggars, charlatans, and buffoons, but I have ignored their disparagement. Rather, in the different cities of Greece and at great religious gatherings in that country, in Asia, in Italy, and in the largest and most populous of the islands, I have patiently listened to old dreams and their consequences. For there was no other possible way in which to get practice in these matters. (13)

As this passage suggests, Artemidorus is keenly aware of the skepticism many people hold toward dream interpretation. He wrote the *Oneirocritica* as a response to that skepticism, trying to demonstrate the legitimacy and practical value of dream interpretation in ordinary people's lives and experiences.

Artemidorus classifies dreams into various types. The first distinction he makes is between *enhypnion* and *oneiros*: "*Oneiros* differs from *enhypnion* in that the first indicates a future state of affairs, while the other indicates a present state of affairs" (14). As examples of *enhypnion*, he describes hungry people dreaming of eating, thirsty people dreaming of drinking, and fearful people dreaming of what they fear. These dreams, Artemidorus says, merely reflect the present condition of the dreamer. *Oneiros*, by contrast, goes beyond the present to "call to the dreamer's attention a prediction of future events" (14).

The second distinction Artemidorus makes is between *theorematic* and *allegorical* dreams. *Theorematic* dreams are direct in their imagery and meaning. An example is a man who dreams of a shipwreck, and then, in waking life, the shipwreck actually happens, exactly as in the dream. *Allegorical* dreams use indirect imagery and symbolism to express their meanings. An example here would be a dream of returning from Hades, which might signify that the dreamer is going to return from a foreign land to his or her own country. Artemidorus says that through allegorical dreams "the soul is conveying something obscurely by physical means" (15). Although he suggests in this passage, and elsewhere in his book, that the source of dreams lies in certain prophetic powers of the soul, Artemidorus declines to engage in debate on this point:

> I do not, like Aristotle, inquire as to whether the cause of our dreaming is outside of us and comes from the gods or whether it is motivated by something within, which disposes the soul in a certain way and causes a natural event to happen to it. Rather, I use the word in the same way that we customarily call all unforeseen things god-sent. (20–21)

The main body of the *Oneirocritica* is an extensive catalog of different dream images and their interpretations. For example, Artemidorus discusses dreams of going blind, of losing teeth, of being beheaded; dreams of various kinds of sexual behavior; dreams of rivers, mountains, clouds, and trees; dreams of kings, priests, gods, and mythological beasts; and on and on and on in remarkably minute and painstaking detail. According to Artemidorus, most dreams have significance for the personal life of the dreamer, relating to the individual's health, family, occupation, romantic relationships, and so forth. He does grant, though, that the dreams of some people (e.g., political leaders) may have significance for the broader community as well.

Some modern psychologists have accused Artemidorus of devising a kind of "cookie cutter" system of dream interpretation in which each dream image is assigned a particular meaning regardless of the dreamer's personal life context. A close reading of the *Oneirocritica* shows, however, that Artemidorus insists any accurate dream interpretation must rely on a detailed knowledge of the dreamer's life: "It is profitable—indeed, not only profitable but necessary—for the dreamer as well as for the person who is interpreting that the dream interpreter know the dreamer's identity, occupation, birth, financial status, state of health, and age" (21). Artemidorus gives numerous examples in which the same dream dreamed by two different people can have two very different interpretations, depending on the particular life circumstances of the dreamers. Furthermore, although he goes to great lengths in the *Oneirocritica* to teach his readers what he knows of the process of dream interpretation, Artemidorus insists that books are not enough: "I maintain that it is necessary for the interpreter of dreams to have prepared himself from his own resources and to use his native intelligence rather than simply to rely upon manuals" (22). Throughout the book, he emphasizes that personal experience is the only reliable guide in the process of dream interpretation:

> I have always called upon experience as the witness and guiding principle of my statements. Everything has been the result of personal experience, since I have not done anything else, and have always devoted myself, day and night, to the study of dream interpretation. (137)

Classic Western Answers to the Three Basic Questions

The views on dreams expressed in the Bible, the philosophy of Aristotle, and the *Oneirocritica* of Artemidorus can be analyzed in terms of the three basic questions of formation, function, and interpretation discussed above.

In the Bible, some dreams are formed directly by God, while other dreams seem to be merely the vain creations of the dreamer's own mind. Dreams serve a number of functions in the Bible: they can be divine revelations, expressions of reassurance and guidance, prophecies of the future, or warnings of possible danger. Dreams can be successfully interpreted by the use of symbolic translations from the dreams' imagery to their waking-life analogs. The best interpreters, Joseph and Daniel, are guided first and foremost by their faith in God. However, the Bible also warns that some dreams can be meaningless and easily misinterpreted, thereby leading people into error and impiety.

In contrast to the Bible's portrait of dream revelations from God, Aristotle asserts that all dreams are formed by the dreamer's own sleep-impaired mind. Dreams have no real function, in Aristotle's view, beyond the small possibility of revealing perceptions of waking life that were overlooked during the day. He grants that dreams can be interpreted, in the sense that resemblances can be discerned between the distorted imagery of a dream and the objects of waking-life perception.

Artemidorus sidesteps the question of how dreams are formed; he is comfortable with either the idea that dreams are literally "god-sent" or the idea that dreams are caused by the human mind alone. Either way, Artemidorus believes that the valuable function of dreams is to foretell what will come in the dreamer's future. For Artemidorus, dreams are important messages that can be used to improve the dreamer's waking life. To interpret dreams, Artemidorus instructs his readers to study all available texts on dreams, to learn as much as possible about the dreamer's personal life, and, most of all, to rely on one's own experience and native intelligence.

Brief as it has been, this review of how dreams have been regarded in three classic Western sources will hopefully give readers a historical context in which they can more fruitfully study and understand the modern psychology of dreaming.

Sigmund Freud Discovers "The Secret of Dreams"

A large hall—numerous guests, whom we were receiving.—Among them was Irma. I at once took her on one side, as though to answer her letter and to reproach her for not having accepted my "solution" yet. I said to her: "If you still get pains, it's really only your own fault." She replied: "If you only knew what pains I've got now in my throat and stomach and abdomen—it's choking me"—I was alarmed and looked at her. She looked pale and puffy. I thought to myself that after all I must be missing some organic trouble.

—Sigmund Freud, July 23–24, 1895 (1965a, 139)

Freud analyzes and interprets this dream of his in chapter 2 of *The Interpretation of Dreams*. (The book's official publication date is 1900, although it actually first appeared in late 1899.) The dream is now known as the "Dream of Irma's Injection" and, because of its seminal importance in the development of Freud's theories, as "the specimen dream of psychoanalysis." Much of Freud's work relied directly on his own dreams and life experiences. To understand his work it is therefore essential to know something about his personal background. This chapter will start with a description of Freud's life up to the writing of *The Interpretation of Dreams*. It will then examine the dream theory that Freud presents in that book, and finally, it will consider some of the additions, changes, and revisions Freud made later in his career to his dream theory. Although it has become reflexive for many people today to attack Freud for being outdated, unscientific, and sexist, the fact remains that virtually all modern dream psychologists have derived their basic principles and techniques from Freud's revolutionary work.

Soon after *The Interpretation of Dreams* was published, Freud wrote a letter to his friend Wilhelm Fliess and described the house (a resort villa outside of Vienna) in which he had experienced his dream of Irma. Freud wrote, "Do you suppose that some day a marble tablet will be placed on the house, inscribed with these words?—'In This House, on July 24th, 1895, the Secret of Dreams was Revealed to Dr. Sigm. Freud.' At the moment there seems little prospect of it" (1965a, 154). Although he did not live to see it, Freud's wish did come true. A marble plaque, inscribed with the exact words Freud had envisioned, was placed at the villa in 1977 (Masson 1985, 418).

Freud's Life

Sigismund Schlomo Freud was born in 1856 in Freiberg, Moravia, to Jacob Freud, a wool merchant, and his third wife, Amalia. As a child, Freud was brought up in a complex network of family relations. Two sons from Jacob's first marriage lived nearby. One of them was older than Freud's relatively young mother, Amalia, and the other was just a year younger than her. Freud's first playmate was his nephew—the little son of his oldest half-brother. In 1860 the family moved to Vienna, where Freud grew up and lived the majority of his life. The outbreak of World War II in 1938 forced him to flee to London, where he died a year later, in 1939.

The Vienna of Freud's youth was an exciting place of optimism and opportunity. In 1867 Jews were officially granted political rights equal to those of other citizens and were increasingly accepted into mainstream society. Throughout his school years, Freud, like many people in the Jewish community, followed the general trend toward cultural assimilation. He embraced the humanistic values of political liberalism, affirmed the universal goals of rationality and human freedom, and identified himself as a German rather than a Jew. But after 1880 the liberal political atmosphere abruptly evaporated. Anti-Semitism returned with a vengeance, and for young Jewish men like Freud, their hopes for assimilation were suddenly shattered, replaced by deep disappointment and bitterness.

Freud entered the University of Vienna in 1873 and graduated in 1881 with a medical degree. From early childhood, he had been deeply interested in scientific pursuits, and he found great pleasure in satisfying his natural curiosity by means of empirical research and investigation. Once out of school, though, Freud was forced to set aside his strong desire for a life of pure medical research. In the spring of 1882, Freud met Martha Bernays, and within two months they were engaged. Freud quickly realized that private practice, not research, was the only realistic road to financial independence and the ability to provide an acceptable home for his future wife. So over the next four years, he slowly built up his medical practice by treating people suffering from hysteria, neuroses, and other mental disturbances. He continued to do as much research as he could, however, and he published several well-received scholarly articles on neurological disorders. Finally, in September of 1886, Sigmund and Martha got married. Between 1887 and 1895, they had six children together.

In 1896 his father died, and the loss pained Freud deeply. He spoke of his sufferings in his numerous letters to Wilhelm Fliess, the ear and nose specialist from Berlin who was Freud's closest friend during those years. In his letters, Freud poured out his emotions, memories, confidences, dreams, anxieties, and wishes, as well as his latest psychological speculations. He told Fliess of the various physical ailments and neurotic symptoms that had been plaguing him, and he confessed, "The chief patient I am preoccupied with is myself" (Masson 1985, 261).

Early in 1898 Freud mentioned to Fliess that he had begun writing a book on dreams. By the fall of 1899, he had completed it, and he sent a copy to Fliess. Freud anxiously wrote, "I have long since become reconciled to [the book] and await its fate in—resigned suspense" (Masson 1985, 380).

The Interpretation of Dreams

In the preface to the second edition of *The Interpretation of Dreams* Freud admitted that his book had great personal significance for him. Looking back on the process of writing it, he found that it was "a portion of my own self-analysis, my reaction to my father's death—that is to say, to the most important event, the most poignant loss, of a man's life" (1965a, xxvi). Further along in his career, when he struggled with doubts about his theories, Freud said that he always regained his confidence by turning back to *The Interpretation of Dreams*. And in 1930, when he reflected on his life's many achievements, he concluded that this book contained "the most valuable of all the discoveries it has been my good fortune to make. Insight such as this falls to one's lot but once in a lifetime" (1965a, xxxii). More than just a statement of his psychological theories, *The Interpretation of Dreams* is a work that expresses Freud's most deeply held feelings and beliefs.

Freud's Method of Interpretation

At the outset of the book, Freud announces his goals: to explain the origins of dream images, to understand the relationship of dreams to other abnormal mental phenomena (like phobias, obsessions, and delusions), and to develop new techniques for treating mental illness. Freud declares that while other psychological researchers have dismissed dreams as the nonsensical products of a sleep-impaired mind, he is going to demonstrate that dreams *do* have psychological meaning and *can* be interpreted.

Two popular methods of interpreting dreams have come down to us through history, Freud says. The first is the symbolic method, which takes the whole dream as a symbolic analogy for a waking-life situation. As an example of this method, Freud cites Joseph's interpretations of Pharaoh's dreams in the Bible. The second is the decoding method, in which a dictionary or manual is used to translate each part of a dream into a known meaning. Freud points to Artemidorus as practicing this method of interpretation. Freud says that both of these traditional methods are arbitrary, subjective, and essentially superstitious. But he insists that modern psychologists are wrong to dismiss dreams as a topic of serious scientific inquiry. Freud says he agrees with the popular traditions that dreams are, if properly interpreted, profoundly meaningful expressions: "I must affirm that dreams really have a meaning and that a scientific procedure for interpreting them is possible" (1965a, 132).

Freud's approach to dream interpretation is similar to the decoding method in that it breaks the dream down into parts and analyzes the meaning of each specific image. But unlike the decoding method, Freud does not translate the dream's images according to the definitions prescribed in an interpreter's manual. Rather, he looks at what occurs to the *dreamer* in relation to each part of the dream. Freud asks the dreamer to "free associate"—to describe whatever thoughts come up in connection to the dream images, no matter how random, foolish, or embarrassing the thoughts might seem. The spontaneous ideas, feelings, and memories that emerge during free association are, Freud claims, the essential clues to the underlying meaning of the dream.

The Dream of Irma's Injection

Freud demonstrates this method by looking at his "Dream of Irma's Injection." He examines this dream very carefully, image by image, and he ponders the meaning of the various thoughts that come into his mind in connection with each element. As he goes on, he notices a recurrent theme beginning to appear: the dream presents a number of different explanations for Irma's pains. First, it is "her own fault" for not listening to Freud. Then her pains are apparently due to some physical disease, and then her troubles are caused by a "dirty syringe" that appears later in the dream. In waking life, Irma was a patient of Freud's, and he had been only partly successful in curing her illness. Some of Freud's medical colleagues (represented in the dream by two of his doctor friends) knew of the case, and Freud worried that they blamed him for Irma's persistent sufferings. But the dream portrays Freud as utterly blameless. In the dream, Irma's pains are not Freud's fault, but are caused by a variety of other things.

At the end of his analysis, Freud concludes that the dream shows how he *wishes* things were: he wishes he were blameless for Irma's pains. The motive for having the dream was this wish, and the dream represents the wish as fulfilled. This, Freud says, is the essence of dreams. This is the secret that was revealed to him at the villa in 1895: *dreams are the fulfillment of wishes.*

Manifest and Latent Contents

The immediate objection to Freud's argument is, but what about nightmares? How could a terrifying dream with intense fear and anxiety possibly be the fulfillment of a wish?

Freud responds by saying that we must distinguish between the *manifest* and the *latent* contents of dreams. The manifest content is the surface of the dream, the images we remember when we awaken. Underlying the dream's surface is the latent content, the deeper thoughts and feelings that Freud says are always expressions of wishes. When a dream is created the latent content becomes transformed in such a way that the underlying wish is heavily distorted, thus masking its original nature. This process of distortion, or censorship, is necessary because the latent wishes are often immoral or antisocial, relating to our basic sexual, aggressive, and egotistical instincts. (In *The Interpretation of Dreams* Freud makes his original statement about the Oedipus complex, the powerful but deeply unconscious yearning in all men to kill their fathers and sleep with their mothers [Freud 1965a, 281–301].) He offers a few examples of dreams whose wishes are obvious and undisguised in the manifest content (e.g., children's dreams and dreams of "convenience," in which a hungry person dreams of eating, a thirsty person dreams of drinking, etc.). However, such obvious dreams are rare, and generally, dreams do disguise their wishes. Freud always denied the popular misunderstanding of his theory that all dreams are motivated by sexual wishes. He says that while sexual wishes do indeed express themselves in dreams, other wishes appear as well (1965a, 194, 432).

In his "Dream of Irma's Injection," the latent content involves deeply self-centered wishes that Freud felt were socially unacceptable. A part of the psyche that Freud calls *the censoring agency* takes such wishes and transforms them in a way that hides their immoral nature.

So one explanation Freud gives for the occurrence of nightmares is that frightening dreams do indeed fulfill wishes: the fear is created by the failure of the censoring agency to mask the wishes well enough. Nightmares are dreams in which the censor's defenses buckle, and the immoral wish succeeds in breaking through during sleep.

Freud also offers a second explanation for frightening dreams. He says that many people have "a masochistic component in [their] sexual constitution," a sense of pleasure in being hurt or humiliated (1965a, 192). For such people, a terribly unpleasant dream could well be fulfilling a wish, a *masochistic* wish.

Freud notes one more possible explanation for why a dream might not appear to be the fulfillment of a wish. He recalls a patient to whom he had explained his theory of dreams. The next day she reported to him a dream of going on vacation with her mother-in-law. In waking life, this woman strongly disliked her mother-in-law and had recently decided to go on vacation by herself. The dream, then, reverses the positive solution she had just reached; it seems to be the exact opposite of what the woman truly wished for. The woman challenged Freud, insisting that her dream proved his theory was wrong. After a moment's pause, Freud responded that the wish motivating her dream was exactly this, to prove him wrong. Freud noted that around the time of the woman's dream he had inferred that she must have suffered an earlier psychological trauma that was partly responsible for her current illness. At first, the woman disputed this, but she later admitted that Freud was right. Her dream was thus motivated by a very deep and powerful wish that Freud was wrong and the earlier trauma had never happened (1965a, 185). Freud goes on to say that readers of his book may have similar "counter-wish dreams" that will apparently disprove Freud's dream theory but will in fact stem from the wish to deny the truth of his ideas about the sexual, aggressive, and egotistical instincts found in all humans.

Based on this analysis of unpleasant feelings in dreams, Freud gives the following definition of the nature of dreams: "A dream is a (disguised) fulfillment of a (suppressed or repressed) wish" (1965a, 194).

The Dream-Work

Looking more carefully at how latent wishes are transformed into the manifest content of the dream, Freud says that two basic sources are used in this process. One source is the "day residue," neutral or indifferent memories from regular day-to-day life. Recent images of ordinary activities are used in dreams as highly effective masks for underlying wishes—like "the sheep's clothing that hides the wolf" (1965a, 216). The other source of material for this process is distant memories from the dreamer's past. Such recollections reach back to the earliest childhood expressions of those powerful instinctual wishes. The deeper the analysis of a dream goes, Freud claims, the closer one comes to the "track of experiences in childhood" that runs throughout the dream's latent content.

The process of transformation itself Freud calls "the dream-work." Freud says that dreams are not, strictly speaking, creative or original in their formation. They are simply a reworking of material already in the psyche. The "essence" of the dream, then, is the dream-work, not the latent wishes and thoughts that have been transformed by it (1965a, 544–545). He describes four specific dream-work mechanisms that change latent thoughts, wishes, and memories into the manifest images of the remembered dream.

The first dream-work mechanism is *condensation*. Freud notes that sometimes the interpretation of a very simple dream image leads to a whole array of complex meanings. What happens, Freud says, is that the dream image serves as a "nodal point" at which many different latent thoughts converge. Looking at another one of his own dreams, the "Dream of the Botanical Monograph," Freud finds that a single dream image—looking through a book he has written—reveals, upon analysis, many different meanings: the dream image relates to a book he had in fact once written, a recent day's memory, his relationship with a colleague, his wife's personal likes and dislikes, and a particular scene from his childhood. All of these latent thoughts are condensed into the manifest dream image of looking through the book. The mechanism of condensation is most evident in dreams with characters that combine the features of two different people (e.g., the face of one person with the hair of another person) or with settings that combine details of two or more different places (e.g., a house from one place set in a different neighborhood or city). Freud found in analyzing his "Dream of Irma's Injection" that the character of Irma represented in condensed form a total of eight different women. Freud says that such dream images are "over-determined"—they contain a multitude of different and complex meanings.

Displacement is the second dream-work mechanism. People often wonder why the emotions they feel in dreams are so often out of sync with what actually happens in the dream. For example, a trivial incident in a dream might make a person cry hysterically or flee in terror or explode in anger. Freud explains these kinds of dreams by saying the dream-work frequently shifts emotions associated with a particular latent thought or wish to a seemingly unrelated dream image. This displacement of emotional intensity is yet another way the dream's latent content is masked. The feelings of sadness, fear, or anger that appear in the dream are not really connected to that trivial manifest image, but are in fact connected to repressed thoughts and wishes in the latent content. In such dreams, the center of emotional intensity has been moved from its original place to a seemingly unimportant location within the dream. (But Freud notes that his dream of Irma's injection does not shift the center of emotional intensity in this way [1965a, 341].)

The third mechanism of the dream-work is what Freud calls the *considerations of representability*. Because dreams are primarily visual experiences, Freud says a major part of the dream-work process involves transforming latent thoughts and wishes into visual images. One example of this would be a dream of a king and queen, which would visually represent latent thoughts about masculine and feminine powers. Another example would be a dream of being chased by a monster, which would visually represent latent thoughts about a frighteningly strong instinctual urge. Freud acknowledges that it is often very difficult to translate a dream's visual images back into the original latent content, but he insists this difficulty is due to the psychological resistance people feel toward the deeply disturbing wishes underlying their dreams. In fact, the dream-work's goal is just this, to prevent those wishes from entering people's awareness. Dreams, Freud says, "are not made with the intention of being understood" (1965a, 377). This explains why we remember so few of our dreams—we do not want to remember them; we resist them.

In the course of representing the latent content in visual images, the dream-work makes extensive use of symbols drawn from the popular culture of the dreamer's social world. Male genitals may be represented in dreams by images of knives, guns, sticks, towers, snakes, and any other long, pointed object. Female genitals may be symbolized by images of boxes, ovens, rooms, ships, and vessels of various kinds. Symbols of sexual intercourse include flying, climbing stairs, riding a train, and any image of up-and-down or back-and-forth movements. Freud notes that these same symbols appear abundantly in mythology, folklore, proverbs, and jokes. In some cases, then, he says the interpreter of a dream can go outside the dreamer's personal associations and find clues to the dream's latent meanings by referring to these common cultural symbols.

The fourth and final dream-work mechanism is *secondary revision*. Secondary revision works to smooth over the rough edges of the manifest dream. It fills in the gaps, makes minor revisions and additions, and generally gives the manifest dream a more orderly appearance. A common instance of this mechanism's work is revealed when a person tries to describe the connection between two different dream scenes. The person might say, "First I was in my home, and then I must have flown, or something like that, to a beach." What has happened, according to Freud, is that two different dream scenes have been made to seem connected. By adding in the vague notion of flying, the dream-work has transformed the two scenes into one dream. This effort to create order and coherence links the dream-work mechanism of secondary revision with the activities of waking thought. Just as people seek order and coherence in their waking perceptions, so do they in dreams. Despite the connotations of its name, Freud insists that this fourth dream-work mechanism does not operate after the other mechanisms have created the dream. Rather, secondary revision works directly on the latent dream material, right alongside the other dream-work mechanisms. (Many years later, however, Freud said that secondary revision occurs once the other dream-work mechanisms have finished performing their functions [1965b, 19–20].) And like those other mechanisms, secondary revision helps to disguise the latent meanings of the dream by strengthening the deceptive façade of the manifest dream. Freud mentions the extreme example of dreams in which the dreamer suddenly thinks, "This is only a dream." Freud says such "dreams within a dream" occur when the censoring agency has failed, and a forbidden wish has broken through. The very rational thought, "this isn't real; I am imagining it," has the effect of diminishing the importance of the dream—and thus fulfills the wish that what has just been dreamed *didn't happen* (1965a, 373–374).

Freud's Model of the Psyche

In the final chapter of *The Interpretation of Dreams* Freud discusses what dreams reveal about the fundamental nature of the human psyche. Having investigated the complex operations of the censoring agency and the four mechanisms of the dream-work, Freud concludes that the "mental apparatus" is composed of three "systems": consciousness, the preconscious, and the unconscious. Consciousness functions to perceive and process information from both external and internal sources.

The preconscious system involves mental operations and processes that are not currently in the field of consciousness but could easily enter awareness if given attention. The unconscious system includes those instincts, wishes, memories, and other mental processes that have been repressed or denied access to the conscious and preconscious systems because of their deeply unsettling nature.

In this "topographical" model of the psyche, the formation of dreams can be explained as follows. When we fall asleep, a conflict soon arises between two different desires: on the one hand, we need the rest that peaceful sleep brings us, and on the other, various unconscious urges take advantage of the weakened power of consciousness in sleep to assert themselves. But those urges are so immoral and disturbing that they threaten to disrupt the person's sleep. So, in order to accommodate both the wish to sleep and the wish to satisfy unconscious urges, the mind (the "psychic apparatus") creates a dream as a compromise. The unconscious urges are transformed by the four mechanisms of the dream-work and are allowed a disguised, hallucinatory fulfillment that prevents their real nature from disturbing sleep. Dreams, Freud says, function as "the guardians of sleep" (1965a, 267).

Ultimately, what the psychological study of dreams reveals is the operation of two fundamentally different modes of human mental functioning. Freud calls them the *primary process* (generally unconscious) and the *secondary process* (generally preconscious and conscious). Primary process thought is instinctual, wishful, and irrational; its sole concern is to seek pleasure. In contrast, secondary process thought is sober, controlled, and rational; it works to regulate the fulfillment of instinctual wishes in accordance with the demands of reality. Primary process thought is infantile and interested in nothing beyond the individual's own wishes and desires. Secondary process thought is mature and aware of the social and physical limits on satisfying those deeper instincts. The thoughts of children, primitives, and people with mental illnesses are governed by the primary process, according to Freud; the thoughts of sane modern adults are governed by the secondary process.

So the "core of our being," in Freud's view, consists of unconscious wishful impulses, of primary process yearnings for pleasure. Secondary process modes of thought develop later, and they help us channel those wishful impulses in more effective ways by means of clear, rational perceptions of reality. Freud believes that this psychological development of ever-greater control of the secondary process over the primary process occurs in each individual's growth from childhood to adulthood and also in the human race's growth from primitive to modern civilization.

A later term Freud uses for this process of channeling and controlling is *sublimation*.

As helpful as dream interpretation may be in treating people with mental illnesses, Freud argues that the greatest value of interpreting dreams lies in the profound insights it gives into the fundamental nature of the human psyche. For this reason, he declares, "The interpretation of dreams is the royal road to a knowledge of the unconscious activities of the mind" (1965a, 647). Freud says that dreams do not give us any knowledge about the future, at least in the sense that ancient peoples believed. Rather, dreams give us greater knowledge of the past, both of the dreamer's childhood and of humankind's primal stages of psychological development. Freud concludes his book by granting that perhaps dreams can be said to lead us into the future—by expressing those powerful and indestructible wishes that do indeed motivate all our life's activities and achievements.

Freud's Later Writings on Dreams

Over the next 40 years of his life, Freud made no fundamental changes to his dream theory. He repeatedly said that nothing had ever persuaded him to alter the basic principles laid out in *The Interpretation of Dreams*. However, he did make dozens of small additions and editorial revisions to the book as a general effort to keep it up to date with new developments in dream research. And in his later writings, he addressed two subjects that were not directly examined in *The Interpretation of Dreams*: post-traumatic dreams and telepathic dreams.

Post-Traumatic Dreams

In his 1920 work *Beyond the Pleasure Principle*, Freud introduced a new view of the psyche, what is often called the "second topography" or the "structural model of the mind" (Gedo and Goldberg 1973). In this new view, the psyche is made up of three "agencies": the *id*, the source of our instinctual energies and desires; the *superego*, the source of internal judgment, criticism, and morality; and the *ego*, which struggles to reconcile the demands of the id and the superego and to adapt the person's desires to the necessities of reality.

Freud developed this new structural model of id-superego-ego in part because the earlier topographical model of unconscious-preconscious-consciousness did not adequately explain post-traumatic dreams. People who have suffered a terrible trauma recently (e.g., in wartime combat) or in the past (e.g., in early childhood) frequently have recurrent dreams that directly replay the traumatic experience, with all the extremely fearful emotions that came with it. Such dreams, Freud realized, did not make sense in terms of the wish-fulfillment theory—what wish could possibly be satisfied by these terrible recurrent nightmares?

Freud acknowledged that traumatic dreams are not fulfilling any instinctual wish for pleasure. Rather, he decided that such dreams are motivated by a wish for mastery, a wish that reflects a more reality-based effort to overcome and control the anxiety arising from the traumatic event. These dreams express a wish not of the id, but of the ego. Freud's new structural model of the psyche allowed him to distinguish dreams generated by purely instinctual wishes (coming from the id) from dreams created in the service of waking-life adaptation (coming from the ego). Post-traumatic dreams, then, are the only exceptions Freud admits to his theory that dreams fulfill repressed instinctual wishes.

Telepathic Dreams

In a number of his later writings, Freud examined the question of whether telepathy is possible in dreams (1953a, 1953b, 1953c, 1965b). Freud was generally suspicious toward all claims to occult knowledge because they appeared to him to be nostalgic efforts to revive religious superstitions in the face of modern scientific progress. Nevertheless, he insisted that telepathy should be investigated like any other phenomenon to determine if it could be empirically verified. So what does a scientific examination reveal about telepathy, the alleged extrasensory perception of other people's thoughts or far-distant events?

Freud studied a number of instances of telepathy in both waking and sleeping states, and he found that many of them could be accounted for by ordinary psychological operations of perception and reasoning. But other cases could not be so easily explained, and here Freud granted that genuinely telepathic, extrasensory modes of perception might be at work. He said that sleep seems to provide an especially good setting for such extrasensory perceptual modes to operate, and the information they convey is transformed by the dream-work just like any other latent content material. While scientists may not yet fully understand how telepathy operates, Freud argues there is no reason to deny it exists or to be frightened by it: "In my opinion it shows no great confidence in science if one does not think it capable of assimilating and working over whatever may perhaps turn out to be true in the assertions of occultists" (1965b, 49).

Freud's Answers to the Three Basic Questions

Freud's answers to the three basic questions about dreams, posed in chapter 1, can be summarized as follows.

Formation

During sleep, unconscious urges, wishes, and thoughts rise up to seek expression and fulfillment. Because this unconscious material is generally immoral and antisocial (relating to sexual, aggressive, and egotistical desires), it threatens to disrupt the individual's ability to sleep restfully. So the unconscious material is halted by a censoring agency in the psyche and transformed by the four mechanisms of the dream-work (condensation, displacement, considerations of representability, and secondary revision). What results is a deceitful manifest dream, put together out of bits and pieces of thoughts, memories, and cultural symbols, that has no apparent connection to the latent wishes and thoughts underlying it. Freud compares a dream's formation to the way in which elaborate new façades were built over ancient Italian churches—the building's public front served as a mask to hide the original structure behind.

Function

In Freud's view, dreams serve two important functions. One is to protect sleep and allow the psychic apparatus to rest peacefully. The other is to provide a partial fulfillment, in hallucinated form, of those powerful unconscious urges, wishes, and desires that rise up during sleep. By gaining some measure of satisfaction through dreams, those unconscious forces put less pressure on waking consciousness; this helps people function more effectively in their daily lives. (In cases where people have suffered extreme traumas, their dreams may serve the ego-related function of mastering anxiety and thus adapting better to reality.)

Interpretation

Dreams are not meant to be understood, Freud says. On the contrary, they are meant to deceive, to hide their true meanings from the dreamer. Furthermore, people actively resist understanding their dreams because those true meanings are so disturbing. Nevertheless, Freud argues that dreams can be interpreted by a process of reversing the dream-work: tearing down the dream's manifest façade, breaking it into pieces, and carefully reconstructing the original thoughts and wishes that motivated the dream's formation. An interpretation of a dream should begin by asking the dreamer to free associate to each image of the dream, describing whatever ideas, feelings, and memories spontaneously arise in connection with those images. At certain points, the interpreter may go outside the dreamer's free associations and rely on the meanings of common cultural symbols to explain particular dream images. Dream interpretation has both practical and theoretical value for Freud. Practically, it aids in the treatment of mentally disturbed people. Theoretically, it gives important insights into the fundamental nature of the human psyche.

C.G. Jung Descends into the Collective Unconscious

I saw a stone stairway leading down [into the ground]. Hesitantly and fearfully, I descended. At the bottom was a doorway with a round arch, closed off by a green curtain. . . . Curious to see what might be hidden behind, I pushed it aside [and saw] a huge thing made of skin and naked flesh. . . . I was paralyzed with terror. At that moment I heard from outside and above me my mother's voice. She called out, "Yes, just look at him. That is the man-eater!"
—C.G. Jung, age 3–4 (Jung 1965, 11–12)

C.G. Jung is, besides Freud, the most influential dream psychologist of the 20th century. Jung was for many years Freud's closest friend and leading student. But they had a bitter falling out (in part over their disagreement about the nature of dreams), and from that point forward, their respective theories developed in sharply different directions. Although zealous Freudians and Jungians battle each other to this day, most dream researchers recognize that both Freud and Jung were deeply insightful and creative psychological pioneers whose works have enduring relevance to the study of dreams.

Like Freud, Jung developed his theories directly out of his own personal dream experiences. In his autobiography, *Memories, Dreams, Reflections* (1965), he says that his intellectual life originated in the process of pondering his dreams. The dream quoted above is the earliest Jung could remember, one that never stopped haunting him. Throughout his life, Jung experienced powerful dreams that inspired, shaped, and guided his psychological research.

As *Memories, Dreams, Reflections* makes clear, Jung's personal life and professional work were intimately connected. This chapter will begin by describing some key aspects of Jung's life—his childhood dreams, his relationship with Freud, and his "confrontation with the unconscious." Then it will outline the basic elements of his theory of dreams and relate that theory to his general model of psychological development.

Jung's Life

Carl Gustav Jung was born in 1875 in a small village near Basel, Switzerland. He was brought up in a sternly Protestant household—his father, Paul, was a country parson and his mother, Emilie, was a minister's daughter. The gloomy religious atmosphere at home, combined with the various physical ills that afflicted everyone in the family, led the young Carl to become absorbed in his own private games, fantasies, and dreams. Jung says that his dream of the frightening "man-eater" in the cave showed him that the Lord Jesus was not the only power in the universe: "Through this childhood dream I was initiated into the secrets of the earth" (1965, 15). The religion of his father could not explain the occurrence of such strange dreams and visions, so Jung gradually developed the idea that there were two personalities living within him—personality number 1, the Swiss schoolboy and son of his parents, and personality number 2, an older, wiser, very mysterious man who came from the distant past.

As he got older Jung decided to study medicine, as a compromise between personality number 1's interest in scientific knowledge and personality number 2's fascination with the mysteries of nature. He soon focused on psychiatry and in 1900 took a post at the Burholzi Mental Hospital in Zurich. These, Jung says, were "the years of my apprenticeship" (1965, 114). The basic challenge of his work at the hospital was to discover what was going on inside his mentally ill patients. He listened carefully to their fantasies, dreams, and hallucinations, and he gradually realized that his patients were not "crazy" but were in fact struggling to answer fundamentally spiritual questions about the meaning of life. Traditional religious symbols, dogmas, and institutions had failed these people, leaving them helpless against external traumas and internal conflicts. Over the years, Jung developed various therapeutic techniques to help his patients find, within their own unconscious selves, new symbols and truths that could relieve their sufferings.

In 1906 Jung, who had read *The Interpretation of Dreams* soon after it was published, sent a complimentary copy of his book on word associations to Freud. Freud wrote back a note of thanks, and soon the two were corresponding regularly. They met face-to-face for the first time in 1907, and according to Jung, they "talked virtually without a pause for thirteen hours" (1965, 149). An intense and deeply ambivalent friendship had begun, one that would have a lifelong impact on both men. Jung quickly became Freud's most energetic and dedicated supporter, and Freud soon began referring to Jung as his chosen successor to lead the onward expansion of the psychoanalytic movement. Jung wrote articles promoting Freud's theories, helped to edit psychoanalytic journals, and worked on building up international organizations of Freud's followers.

But Jung says that from the start of their friendship he had uncomfortable feelings about Freud's emphasis on sexuality and his skepticism toward religion. As Jung began writing a new book, *Symbols of Transformation*, which challenged Freud on these points, he worried their friendship would not survive the book's publication. Jung was right: when the work appeared in 1912, Freud felt betrayed by the person who was supposed to carry psychoanalysis victoriously into the future. Their letters to each other became increasingly angry, indignant, and scornful. By 1914 Jung and Freud broke off all relations with each other.

Now began what Jung called "a period of inner uncertainty" and what some of his biographers interpret as a "creative illness" (Ellenberger 1970, Homans 1979). His bitter break with Freud led to a general withdrawal from the professional world. Jung resigned from all psychoanalytic associations, stopped reading scientific books and articles, and gave up his teaching position at the University of Zurich. For the next several years, he was besieged by strange thoughts, visions, and dreams that he felt dreadfully incapable of understanding: "I stood helpless before an alien world" (1965, 177). Despite the pain and confusion he was experiencing, Jung decided to surrender to these unconscious impulses erupting within him and do his best to make sense of them. He regarded these years of "confrontation with the unconscious" as a scientific experiment, as an investigation into the darkest depths of the individual psyche. He allowed himself to play childish games, wrote out all his dreams and fantasies in exhaustive detail, and made elaborate drawings and paintings of especially haunting images. Using his family and his work at the hospital as anchors in social reality, Jung slowly learned to differentiate himself from these powerful images bursting out of the unconscious. This enabled him to bring them into relationship with his consciousness.

This long inner crisis came to a close by 1918, and what followed was "the Work"—Jung's major psychological writings. He took the dream and fantasy experiences of 1912–1918 as the *"prima materia"* for all his later research and theorizing: "It has taken me virtually forty-five years to dis-till within the vessel of my scientific work the things I experienced and wrote down at that time (Jung 1965, 199). His psychological theories were devoted to communicating in scientific language what he had learned from the unconscious material that flooded through him during the years that followed his break with Freud.

Jung's Theory of Dreams

Jung did not write one great, systematic work on dreams, comparable to Freud's *The Interpretation of Dreams*. Rather, he discussed dreams in nearly everything he wrote, from *Two Essays on Analytical Psychology* (the first major work following his 1912–1918 crisis) to his final testament in *Memories, Dreams, Reflections*. The basic elements of his dream theory can be summarized as follows.

The Naturalness of Dreams

In Jung's view, dreams are the direct and natural expression of the cur-rent condition of the dreamer's inner world. Jung rejects Freud's claim that dreams intentionally disguise their meanings, and he dismisses the psychoanalytic distinction between a dream's manifest and latent con-tents. Jung believes that dreams give an honest self-portrayal of the psyche's actual state. He says that "to me dreams are a part of nature, which harbors no intention to deceive, but expresses something as best as it can, just as a plant grows or an animal seeks food as best it can" (1965, 161–162). Dreams appear strange not because of the trickery of a deceitful censor but because our conscious minds do not always understand the special symbolic language of the unconscious. If we want to discover what dreams mean, Jung argues, we must learn to speak their distinctive language of image, symbol, and metaphor.

Compensatory and Prospective Functions

Among the many functions that dreams serve (and he acknowledges there are a number of different ones), there are two that Jung considers especially important. The first relates to the central process of *compensa-tion*, which Jung believes governs the relationship between consciousness and the unconscious. Whereas Freud puts great emphasis on the develop-ment of rational consciousness, Jung argues that psychological health and development involve a progressive balancing of consciousness with the unconscious, with the more "irrational" aspects of the psyche. "We can take the theory of compensation as a basic law of psychic behavior," he says (1974, 101). Dreams are a powerful means of promoting the overall balance of the psyche because they bring forth unconscious contents that the conscious ego has either ignored, not valued sufficiently, or actively repressed.

In *Memories, Dreams, Reflections* Jung gives a personal example of a compensatory dream. He had realized, during an analysis with a female patient, that his dialogue with her was becoming increasingly shallow. Something was wrong, but he didn't know what it could be. So he decided to raise the issue with her in their next session. The night before that session, Jung had a dream: he is walking down a valley, with a steep hill on his right. On the top of the hill is a castle, and on the highest tower he sees a woman. In order to see her clearly, he has to bend his head far back. At this point Jung woke up from the dream with a painful crick in the back of his neck. He immediately recognized the woman as his patient and thus realized what the dream meant: "If in the dream I had to look up at the patient in this fashion, in reality I had probably been looking down on her. Dreams are, after all, compensations for the conscious attitude" (1965, 133). When Jung told his patient of the dream and his interpretation, he found that it produced an immediate and positive change in the therapeutic relationship.

The second valuable function of dreams, according to Jung, is to provide *prospective* visions of the future. He agrees with Freud that dreams may look backward to past experiences, but he argues that dreams also look forward to anticipate the dreamer's future development. Jung did not mean that all dreams necessarily predict the future, only that dreams frequently suggest what might happen, what potential and possibilities the dreamer's future might hold.

Jung himself experienced a number of dreams that he believed accurately foretold future occurrences both in his personal life and in society. For example, in the fall of 1913 he had an hour-long vision of an ocean of blood rushing over the Alps mountain range and drowning all of Europe. Then, in the spring of 1914, he had a series of dreams in which an Arctic cold wave descended upon Europe and froze it to ice; all living things were killed by the frost (Jung 1965, 176). Just a few months after these dreams, World War I broke out.

Methods of Interpretation

Jung says that an analyst must start the interpretation of any dream with an admission of ignorance and a willingness to find something new—the interpreter must be open to whatever the dream has to say. Jung recommends that the first step should be to examine, in as much detail as possible, the dream's context in the individual's waking life. (Ideally, the dreamer has provided a series of dreams, for this will provide a broader picture of the individual's unconscious world than can be gained from a single dream.) Then, Jung says the analyst should seek *amplifications* of the dream's images and themes. Unlike Freud's process of free association, which Jung believes leads the dreamer away from the dream, amplification involves circling around the dream's images again and again, in an effort to discover deeper elements of the dream's meanings. If a man dreams about a tall tree, for instance, he might free associate about his garden, a nearby park, a childhood experience climbing a tree, and so forth. All of this is interesting, Jung says, but not necessarily relevant to the dream about the tall tree. Jung would encourage the dreamer to describe in detail how the tree in the dream appeared, how it was shaped, and what color its leaves were. He would ask the dreamer what trees are like in general, how they grow, what nourishes them, and what threatens them. He would ask how the tall tree makes the dreamer feel, what emotions come up in the dream—each of these questions works to keep the dreamer focused directly on the dream itself and on the complex web of meanings expressed in the image of the tall tree.

To help the dreamer in this process of amplification, Jung will sometimes note the parallels between a particular dream image and similar images in world mythology. In this example of the dream of the tall tree, such parallels might include the Tree of Knowledge, which the Bible describes as standing in the Garden of Eden; the ever-verdant ash tree, Yggdrasil, which Nordic mythology says is rooted at the center of the world; and the Tree of Life, which in the Jewish mystical tradition of Kabbalah represents the divine ordering of the cosmos. Jung would bring up these parallels not to define what the dream means, but to give the dreamer new perspectives on that particular image of the tall tree.

One important question Jung asks in interpreting a dream is whether the dream's images and symbols relate primarily to the *objective* level of meaning or to the *subjective* level. To take a new example, a dream of fighting with an angry man might relate to an actual experience the dreamer had the previous day of arguing with an angry man; Jung would call this interpretation on the objective level. The same dream could also relate to an emotional conflict within the dreamer, a conflict with "angry man" elements of the dreamer's own psyche; Jung would call this interpretation on the subjective level. More often than not, Jung focuses his attention on the subjective aspects of a dream. He once compared dreams to a "theater in which the dreamer is himself the scene, the player, the prompter, the producer, the author, the public, and the critic. . . . [The subjective approach] conceives all the figures in the dream as personified features of the dreamer's own personality" (1974, 52). So if the dream of fighting with the angry man had taken place inside a bank with a crowd watching, Jung would suggest that every element in the dream—the angry man, the bank, the crowd—represents some element within the dreamer's psyche. Jung expands on this idea of dreams as an internal theatrical play by saying that each dream can be analyzed into four dramatic components: an opening scene, the development of a plot, the emergence of a conflict, and the resolution (2008).

Another method Jung uses in interpreting a dream is called *active imagination*. In this process, Jung asks a patient to sit quietly and concentrate on reimagining the dream in all its details. Gradually, the dream's images, characters, and feelings come to life again, opening up new meanings and insights to the dreamer. The key to active imagination is allowing the unconscious free access to consciousness, thereby enabling the dream to continue its dramatic unfolding. Jung likens the process to "dreaming the dream onward."

The practice of dream interpretation should, in Jung's view, be a matter of "joint reflection," a "dialectical process" in which both the analyst and the dreamer participate. The only legitimate criterion for a valid interpretation is its therapeutic value: if the interpretation brings forth meanings that help the dreamer, then it is a valid interpretation. Jung says in an article titled "The Aims of Psychotherapy,"

> It ought not matter to me whether the result of my musings on the dream is scientifically verifiable or tenable, otherwise I am pursuing an ulterior— and therefore autoerotic—aim. I must content myself wholly with the fact that the result means something to the patient and sets his life in motion again. I may allow myself only one criterion for the result of my labors. Does it work? (1966, 42–43)

Symbols, Archetypes, and the Collective Unconscious

The interpretation of symbols is central to Jung's approach to dreams. On the one hand, he says there are no fixed meanings to any symbols— all dream symbols must be related to the dreamer's unique waking-life situation. But on the other hand, he believes that dreams regularly contain *archetypal* symbols, whose meanings are universal, transcending the dreamer's individual consciousness. Jung's interpretations of dreams leave the realm of the individual's associations entirely when he discerns the presence of such archetypal symbols.

Jung had a dream in 1909 that gave him what he says was his first clear perception of the universal, transpersonal realms of the psyche. It came while he was traveling with Freud on a steamship bound for the United States. The two men had been invited to Clark University in Massachusetts to receive honorary degrees, and during the long voyage across the Atlantic, they spent many hours interpreting each other's dreams. One night Jung had a dream in which he finds himself in the second story of a house that he feels is *his* house. He goes downstairs, and when he reaches the ground floor, he sees that all the furniture and decorations date from medieval times. He then follows a stone stairway down another floor to the cellar, which he discovers is a dwelling from ancient Rome. He sees a stone slab on the floor, opens it, and descends into a dark cave, strewn with bones and the remains of a primitive culture. On the dusty floor of the cave he sees two human skulls, very old and half-disintegrated (1965, 157–161).

He shared this dream with Freud, who insisted the two skulls represent some powerful wish. Jung sensed the wish Freud had in mind was a secret death wish, but Jung felt a "violent resistance" to such an interpretation (1965, 161). Instead, he saw the dream as a revelation of a "collective *a priori* beneath the personal psyche"—a realm of the unconscious that reaches far beyond the individual's personal life (1965, 161). For Jung, the dream was a "structural diagram of the human psyche" showing that below the *personal unconscious* of our memories and experiences, there is a *collective unconscious* that connects us at a fundamental level with the whole evolutionary history of humankind.

The claim that dreams express not just personal contents but also collective contents is one of the most distinctive features of Jung's dream theory. Archetypes, Jung explains, are universal psychic images that structure human mental functioning. They are inherited patterns of thought that the human mind uses to frame perceptions, experiences, and feelings. Jung insists that archetypes are not themselves specific images, but are rather blueprints for images—with the actual content to be filled in with material from the individual's life. Archetypal symbols reflect a natural wisdom ingrained deeply within the human unconscious, and when they appear in dreams, they can provide the dreamer with especially profound insights and guidance. Jung found that the world's religious and mythological traditions contain a wealth of archetypal images, symbols, and themes, and he recommended that anyone intending to practice dream interpretation should make a detailed study of these traditions.

Among the most common archetypes described by Jung in his writings are the persona, the shadow, the anima and animus, and the Self.

The *persona* archetype represents the basic human need to present ourselves favorably in society. Jung frequently likens the persona to a mask we put on when we appear in public—the persona is necessary both to protect vulnerable aspects of the individual's personality and to promote the smooth, efficient functioning of community life. A dream of behaving inappropriately in a social situation might indicate that the dreamer's persona is weak, that the mask is in danger of falling off. A dream of being trapped at a party might indicate the mask has become too tightly attached, and the dreamer cannot separate social appearances from his or her own identity.

The *shadow* archetype represents all those unconscious elements and energies of the psyche that are poorly integrated with the individual's consciousness. These elements may be separated from consciousness, but they are still connected to it and follow the individual around "like a shadow." Jung characterized the shadow as a dark "other" within us, the primitive, instinctual aspects of ourselves that challenge the dominance of light, civilization, and consciousness. However, the shadow may, in some cases, express the brighter or more positive aspects of an individual's personality. For example, a violent criminal who has overly actualized the psyche's aggressive energies may have dreams filled with shadow images of kindness, nurturance, and altruism. The shadow archetype typically appears in nightmares, especially nightmares in which the dreamer is being chased by a frightening animal, monster, or vengeful murderer. Such terrifying dreams reveal that the individual's conscious attitude is in conflict with the shadow elements of his or her unconscious. The dreamer's task is then to confront those elements, understand them, and try to integrate them with consciousness.

The *anima* archetype represents the female aspects of a man's psyche, and the *animus* archetype represents the male aspects of a woman's psyche. All people, Jung claims, carry within them biological and psychological elements of the opposite sex. The anima and animus archetypes express the relationship of those elements to the individual's conscious personality. Our parents provide the original material out of which anima and animus images are formed; social ideals about the proper gender roles of men and women provide further material. The anima and animus appear in dreams to help people create psychological balance between the feminine and masculine energies within them. Jung says these archetypes can also represent "soul-images," serving as potential mediators or guides in the individual's efforts to integrate consciousness and the unconscious.

The archetype of the *Self* represents the human potential to achieve wholeness and self-realization, to unite all the psychological opposites into a harmonious totality. Although such complete wholeness is rarely achieved, Jung says the archetype of the Self exists to remind us that it is a genuine potential within our psyches. Images of the Self are frequently expressed, both in dreams and in religious traditions, by *mandalas*. Mandalas are pictorial designs with intricately symmetrical patterns surrounding an accentuated center. Many mandalas take the form of flowers, crosses, and wheels. The number four, Jung finds, is a universally recurrent element in their design. When mandala imagery appears in a dream, it generally addresses the dreamer's current relationship to his or her own potential for psychological wholeness. A dream of four trees in which three of the trees are tall and healthy while the fourth is short and sickly might suggest that one element of the dreamer's potential wholeness needs to be given greater attention and nurturance.

Jung's Views on Individuation, Religion, and Modern Society

Mandala imagery in dreams reveals what Jung believes is the ultimate nature and function of dreaming: to promote the basic evolutionary process of bringing consciousness and the unconscious into balance, wholeness, and integration—the process he calls *individuation*. Individuation is the "complete actualization of the whole human being" (1974, 108). It represents, Jung says, the true and final goal of all life. A common misunderstanding of this central concept in Jung's psychology is that individuation means rejecting consciousness and giving free rein to the unconscious. Jung repeatedly emphasizes that consciousness has the vital task of actualizing the contents that rise up from the unconscious—neither controlling nor surrendering to them but integrating them into a broader, more balanced, conscious self-awareness. "In the final analysis," Jung says, "the decisive factor is always consciousness, which can understand the manifestations of the unconscious and take up a position towards them" (1965, 187).

As dream experiences demonstrate, the individuation process unfolds naturally within the life of each human being. Throughout history this process has been encouraged, guided, and nurtured by the world's religious and mythological traditions. Jung believes that religions have always served to promote the union of consciousness and the unconscious. The individuation process is at the core of all sacred teachings, from the mythic lore of the Australian Aborigines and Native Americans to the grand theological systems of Christians and Buddhists. Jung devotes many of his writings to detailed analyses of the archetypal symbolism to be found in world religions. He gives special attention to Gnosticism, a first-century CE merging of Greek mysticism with early Christianity, and alchemy, a medieval tradition of natural philosophy. Jung argues that Gnostics and alchemists already knew what modern psychologists are just now discovering about the deepest realms of the unconscious.

Jung believes that traditional religious beliefs, symbols, and rites no longer function effectively for many people in modern Western society. The rise of rational science, the growing power of technology, and the ever-increasing complexity of modern life have all combined to tear people away from their roots in religious and mythological traditions. As a result, increasing numbers of people are suffering from dangerous psychological imbalances. The more humans have developed their powers of reason, the more they have ignored or repressed the irrational elements within their psyches. Jung says the 20th century's bloody history of warfare proves that our great advances in civilization have not eliminated but have actually provoked these destructive outbursts of primitive aggression.

The goal of modern psychotherapy, in Jung's view, is to perform the services that religious traditions used to perform: helping people find their own balanced wholeness, their own path toward individuation. Dreams are an invaluable resource in psychotherapy because they show both the present condition of the dreamer's psychological development and the future possibilities of growing toward greater self-integration. In one of his case studies, Jung makes a lengthy analysis of a patient's dreams, examining the many parallels between the dream series and images from ancient myths, spiritual traditions, and mystical teachings. The case demonstrates that modern individuals, no matter how rational, civilized, and secular they have become, will still find unconscious yearnings that are essentially religious toward personal wholeness. Jung says this case "proves that even if the conscious mind is miles away from the ancient conceptions of the rites of renewal, the unconscious still strives to bring them closer in dreams" (1974, 211).

Indeed, Jung believes that it is precisely because modern people have an overly rational worldview that religious compensations emerge in our dreams, working to balance that one-sided conscious outlook. While religious compensations through what Jung calls *big dreams* are rare, their power and influence can be tremendous: "Big dreams . . . are often remembered for a lifetime, and not infrequently prove to be the richest jewel in the treasure-house of psychic experience" (1974, 76). However, Jung repeatedly warns that people should not underestimate the real dangers that face anyone who truly descends into the depths of the unconscious. Jung tells the story of an apparently normal man who came to Zurich wanting to be trained as an analyst. After several weeks of failing to remember any dreams, the man finally had a dream that he shared with Jung. In the dream, the man takes a train to a city. He wanders through the streets and comes to an area filled with medieval buildings. He goes inside one, gets dreadfully lost, and finally stumbles into a large, dark room—and in the middle of the room he finds an idiot child, about two years old, smeared with its own feces. The man told Jung he awoke from this dream in a panic. When Jung heard the dream, he immediately recognized it as an indication of a latent psychosis; the man was in grave danger of losing conscious control to the terribly primitive, childlike forces hidden within him. Jung politely but firmly discouraged the man from further analytic training. This case, Jung says, shows that people should be very careful when stirring up the unconscious. With this man, "his emphatic normality reflected a personality which would not have been developed but simply shattered by a confrontation with the unconscious" (1965, 136).

Jung's Answers to the Three Basic Questions

Formation

Dreams are formed out of material from the personal unconscious (e.g., thoughts, feelings, and experiences from daily life) and from the collective unconscious (e.g., the archetypes of the persona, shadow, anima and animus, and Self). The rich imagery and complex symbolism of dreams is simply the natural means by which the unconscious expresses itself. Dreams do not intentionally hide their meanings, but rather express themselves honestly and directly, in the best way they can. Jung believes the ultimate power behind the formation of dreams comes from a transpersonal realm far beyond the individual's own psyche.

Function

The major function of dreams is to compensate for the imbalances of the conscious personality. Dreams bring forth unconscious elements of the psyche that the individual has ignored or repressed; dreams challenge the individual to integrate those elements with consciousness and thus develop a deeper, more balanced self-awareness. A second important function of dreaming is to provide prospective visions of future potential in the dreamer's life. Overall, the function of dreams is to promote the basic psychological process of individuation, the individual's natural yearning to grow toward ever-greater wholeness and self-actualization.

Interpretation

As expressions of a natural psychological process, dreams do not need to be consciously interpreted and understood in order to fulfill their functions. However, Jung believes these functions can be greatly enhanced by the practice of dream interpretation. Jung's method is first to clarify the dream's context in the waking-life situation of the dreamer and then to seek *amplifications* of the dream's imagery: carefully circling around the dream, gradually discovering the complex web of meanings and emotions expressed by each particular image. The practice of amplification frequently draws on the world's religious and mythological traditions to provide further insights into the dream's meanings. Jung looks at how the dream may relate to the dreamer's activities in the objective reality of external society, and how the dream's characters, settings, and events may represent subjective aspects of the individual's inner world. The conscious interpretation of dreams, especially a series of dreams, has tremendous value for psychotherapy because it powerfully stimulates the process of individuation. Especially for modern Westerners, dream interpretation can be a potent means of reconnecting their rational, conscious selves with the irrational, unconscious elements of their psychic depths.

Alternative Clinical Theories about Dreams

Goebbels was visiting my factory. He had all the workers line up in two rows facing each other. I had to stand in the middle and raise my arm in the Nazi salute. It took me half an hour to get my arm up, inch by inch. Goebbels showed neither approval nor disapproval as he watched my struggle, as if it were a play. When I finally managed to get my arm up, he said just five words—"I don't want your salute"—then turned and went to the door. There I stood in my own factory, arm raised, pilloried right in the midst of my own people. I was only able to keep from collapsing by staring at his clubfoot as he limped out. And so I stood until I woke up.

—60-year-old German factory owner, 1936 (Beradt 1966, 5)

A Freudian interpretation of this dream would seek personal associations to each of the dream's parts and trace the associations back to repressed unconscious wishes. The image of Joseph Goebbels, the notorious minister of culture for the Nazi regime, would likely be interpreted as a father figure, with the slow, painful raising of the arm symbolizing the dreamer's feelings of impotence and Oedipal anxiety. A Jungian interpretation, by contrast, would try to amplify the dream's elements and would look to see if the unconscious is compensating for imbalances in the dreamer's conscious attitudes. The humiliation the factory owner suffers in the dream might be an unconscious corrective to excessive pride and arrogance in his waking life, and the evil Goebbels might be a shadow figure representing the violent, totalitarian forces in his own psyche.

Are these the only two ways of psychologically approaching a dream? Many people have assumed that Freud and Jung simply *are* the psychology of dreaming: there is Freud's theory, there is Jung's theory, and then there are minor commentaries on them. In one sense, this assumption is valid. No one has written a book to rival Freud's *The Interpretation of Dreams*, and no one has probed the universe of dream symbolism as deeply as Jung did. However, the theories of Freud and Jung do not exhaustively answer all of the important questions about dreaming. A number of psychologists have learned from Freud and Jung and then gone on to develop alternative approaches to dreaming, approaches based on different theoretical frameworks and different clinical practices.

This chapter will describe five major clinical theories about dreams that arose after Freud and Jung: the Individual Psychology of Alfred Adler, the Existential Psychoanalysis of Medard Boss, the Ego Psychology of Thomas French and Erika Fromm, the Gestalt Psychology of Frederick Perls, and the Cognitive-Experiential approach of Clara Hill. These are by no means the only alternatives to Freud and Jung, but they are certainly among the most innovative and influential of alternative dream theories.

Individual Psychology: Alfred Adler

Alfred Adler was a Viennese doctor who became one of the earliest members of Freud's psychoanalytic circle. From 1902 to 1911 he wrote several papers on Freudian theory and participated actively in the newly founded Viennese Psychoanalytic Society. In 1910 he was elected to be the group's president. But eventually Adler and Freud realized their views diverged on many key theoretical issues. In 1911 Adler resigned from Freud's group and formed his own organization, which he called the Society for Individual Psychology. He wrote and taught extensively through the rest of his career and had a large, but often unacknowledged, influence on many later schools of psychology.

Adler's approach to dreams starts with the basic assertion that all humans have an innate drive to preserve the unity of their personalities: "The supreme law of both life-forms, sleep and wakefulness alike, is this: the sense of worth of the self shall not be allowed to be diminished" (1956, 358). Adler refers to this innate, dynamic drive as a striving to achieve *superiority* (in the sense of freedom, security, power) and, conversely, to overcome *inferiority*.

> In every psychological phenomenon [there is] the striving for superiority.
> It runs parallel to physical growth and is an intrinsic necessity of life itself.

It lies at the root of all solutions of life's problems and is manifested in the way in which we meet these problems. All our functions follow its direction. . . . The urge from below to above never ceases. Whatever premises all our philosophers and psychologists dream of—self-preservation, pleasure principle, equalization—all these are but vague representations, attempts to express the great upward drive. (103)

The various behaviors that each person uses to defend this sense of superiority and self-worth make up what Adler calls "the individual's style of life" (358).

In sharp contrast to Freud and Jung, Adler argues that consciousness and the unconscious are not opposed to each other; they are fundamentally united, in that both express the individual's style of life. Adler therefore concentrates exclusively on how dreams relate to the individual's day-to-day existence, rather than using dreams to delve into the deep unconscious realms of the psyche. At the most basic level, then, Adler considers dreams valuable because they are a diagnostic tool that psychotherapists can use to learn about the characteristic pattern of behaviors, beliefs, and attitudes that a patient uses to preserve his or her personal integrity and style of life.

To interpret dreams, Adler relies first on the free association method of Freud, eliciting from the dreamer whatever thoughts and memories arise in connection with the dream. Adler also follows Freud in looking very carefully at the dream's emotional content, because he believes the emotions a person feels in a dream can reveal key elements of his or her particular style of life. But Alder departs from Freud on the issue of universal symbols. He says, "We must modify each dream interpretation to fit the individual concerned; and each individual is different. . . . The only valid dream interpretation is that which can be integrated with an individual's general behavior, early memories, [and] problems" (363).

Adler grants that dreams serve a kind of problem-solving function, but in his view, this function is deceptive and ultimately ineffectual. When a person faces a problem in waking reality that challenges the resources of his or her style of life, a dream will respond by metaphorically reworking the problem until it can be solved using the person's ordinary coping strategies. For instance, a woman who was dissatisfied with her family life might have a dream in which she criticizes her husband for failing to take care of their children. In Adler's view, such a dream would have taken a life problem the woman had been unable to solve (her general unhappiness with family life) and transformed it into a more limited problem that she *could* solve (by casting her husband as an incompetent father). Adler says, "In dreams we fool ourselves into an inadequate solution of a problem, inadequate from the standpoint of common sense, but adequate from the standpoint of our style of life" (360). Dreams are essentially self-protective fantasies that reduce our problems to a size we feel we can manage.

For Adler, then, dreaming is a product of failed adaptation to the waking world. Dreams occur when there is a conflict between a person's style of life and the demands of "reality and common sense"; they are "self-deceptions" that try desperately to preserve the person's sense of unity and self-worth (360). But because the aim of Individual Psychology is to increase an individual's courage to meet the problems of life, Adler's basic approach to dreams is to use them as illustrations of where the person is weakest and in most need of developing greater rational judgment. Indeed, Adler suggests that people who deal adequately with their problems in the daytime do not need to dream at all: "We should expect, therefore, that the more the individual goal agrees with reality, the less a person dreams; and we find that it is so. Very courageous people dream rarely, for they deal adequately with their situation in the daytime" (360). One commentator has noted that Adler seems to have dreamed very little himself, remarking, "It sounds very much as if Adler adapted his theory to accommodate the fact that at some point he personally stopped remembering his dreams" (Shafton 1995, 138).

Existential Psychoanalysis: Medard Boss

Medard Boss was a Swiss psychoanalyst who, following his training in Freudian clinical practice, worked for ten years with Jung in Zurich. But, as he says in the preface to his major work, *The Analysis of Dreams*, he gradually realized that Freud, Jung, and all the other leading dream psychologists were making the same faulty assumption: "[T]hey replaced the immediate and direct phenomenon by explanations of it. They saw in dreams the expression of something else, something merely assumed to exist behind the phenomena, some mental construct" (1958, 9). Boss decided what was needed was greater attention to "the dream phenomenon itself," apart from all theories and hypotheses and clinical models. He became very interested in the work of Ludwig Binswanger, who—as founder of the *Daseineanalyse*, or existentialist approach to psychology— had been working to integrate Freudian psychoanalysis with the thought of German philosopher Martin Heidegger. After making his own careful study of Heidegger's work, particularly Heidegger's central concept of "being-in-the-world" (*Dasein*), Boss developed his own distinctive existentialist approach to dreams.

Boss, like Adler, rejects the idea that consciousness and the unconscious are two radically different and mutually opposed aspects of the psyche. But unlike Adler, Boss uses a sophisticated philosophical framework to support and develop his position. For Boss, the unity of conscious and unconscious life is based on the primary ontological fact that we always exist in relationship with things and people. We *are* these relationships; they constitute our being and reality. Humans do not possess any essence or nature that can be identified outside of our relationships, outside of our being-in-the-world. Boss further argues this basic philosophical truth applies to all our experiences: waking life and dreaming life are but different aspects of our existential relatedness to the world.

Boss draws three important implications regarding dreams from existentialist philosophy. The first is that dreams are real experiences, real in the sense of expressing a genuine mode of being-in-the-world. For this reason, Boss believes dreams deserve no less attention and respect than we give to our waking-life experiences. The second implication is that when we try to understand dreams we must set aside all assumptions and look at the dreams themselves, exactly as they present themselves to us. Boss rejects Freud's manifest/latent content distinction and Jung's method of amplification; in both cases, he says, the dream experience itself is obscured by the interpreter's theoretical biases and expectations. What Boss calls for is an exclusive focus on what the dreamer does, feels, and thinks in the dream, in that particular mode of being-in-the-world he or she experiences while dreaming.

The third implication regards the question of dream symbolism. Boss argues that dreams do not "symbolize" anything, but rather involve real experiences. For example, he would regard a vivid dream of flying as a genuine actualization of the dreamer's innate human potential for freedom. Boss believes that talking about what such a dream symbolizes (e.g., sexuality, ego inflation) only leads the dreamer away from the tangible experience he or she felt within the dream.

In *The Analysis of Dreams*, Boss recounts the story of one of his patients, a male engineer in his 40s who came to Boss for psychotherapy because of depression and sexual impotence. The engineer told Boss he had never dreamed once in his entire life—until two days before their first analytic session. In this dream, the engineer is imprisoned in a dungeon whose bars are made of mathematical signs and numbers. After the analysis began, the engineer brought new dreams to every session. Boss noticed that during the first six and a half months the engineer only dreamed of machines, cars, planes, and electronic devices. Then, for the first time, he dreamed of a living creature—a potted plant. Four months later, the engineer began dreaming of insects, all of them dangerous and harmful. After that, he dreamed for a time of toads, frogs, and snakes. The first mammal to appear in the engineer's dreams was a mouse, which scurried down a hole the instant it was seen. Next were dreams of pigs and then horses and lions. After two years of analysis, the engineer finally dreamed of a human being. In that dream, he discovered a giant unconscious woman, in a long, blood-red dress, trapped under the ice of a frozen pond. Terrified, he ran for help. Six months later, the engineer dreamed he was dancing at a party with the vibrant woman dressed in a similar blood-red outfit, and they fell in passionate love with each other.

Boss reports the engineer's depression had begun diminishing at the time of the potted plant dream, and his sexual potency returned at the time of his dreams of horses and lions. The engineer's dreams revealed that his depression and impotence were ultimately caused by his being a prisoner of "his life-denying mathematical thought. . . . In these dreams he became aware of his imprisonment with a clarity which far surpassed that of waking life" (115). Boss believes dreams both mirror our present being-in-the-world and open us to future possibilities. He describes the dream of a very promiscuous businessman who, though raised a Protestant, was a cynical atheist in adulthood. In his dream, the businessman goes to a monastery built high above a river and talks with a "high Catholic priest" about buying the monastery. The priest cannot speak for long, however, because he has to go say Mass. As the priest departs, the businessman suddenly notices his robes, which are "glowing with indescribable beauty" (144). Boss says that while this man's waking existence had been dominated by "the animality of sexual behavior," his dreaming existence was able to perceive with greater clarity the existence of "higher regions." Boss explains, "New possibilities of being have opened up to him. Into the dream world of this atheist there is suddenly admitted a high Catholic priest. With the appearance of this priest a door to the religious sphere is opened for the dreamer" (144).

Transformative experiences of new possibility come forth in dreams because of the tremendous freedom we have in the dreaming mode of our being-in-the-world. This is why dreams are so valuable in psychotherapy, because they point to those places in people's lives where they are most constricted. Dreams help people discover their innate capacity for free choice and action. Beyond this practical usefulness in psychotherapy, dreams disclose people's most sublime potentials for growth. Boss says we should pay special attention to extremely unusual dream phenomena, for such experiences bring forth radically new possibilities of being-in-the-world. Extrasensory dreams that predict illnesses and accidents, dreams-within-dreams that challenge the nature of personal identity, ecstatic dreams that bring people into connection with the Divine—while some psychologists argue that such dreams are impossible, Boss argues that it is precisely in extraordinary dream experiences like these that we most fully recognize and actualize our true existential freedom.

Ego Psychology: Thomas French and Erika Fromm

Ego Psychology is a branch of psychoanalysis that draws its inspiration from Freud's later writings about the ego's capacity to master both internal and external realities. Analysts like Anna Freud (Freud's youngest daughter), Heinz Hartmann, and Erik Erikson developed Freud's ideas into a new psychotherapeutic approach that puts special emphasis on strengthening the patient's ego—helping it defend against anxiety, control unruly instinctual impulses, and successfully adapt to the demands of social reality. Although Erikson wrote an excellent paper in which he offers a new interpretation of Freud's "Dream of Irma's Injection," the most influential work on dreams from the Ego Psychology perspective has been done by Thomas French and Erika Fromm. Both were classically trained psychoanalysts, and they collaborated on a number of articles about dreams and on the book *Dream Interpretation: A New Approach* (1964).

French and Fromm do not dispute Freud's original dream theory so much as reorient it, pointing it toward the practical waking-life situation of the dreamer's ego. They view every dream as an attempt by the ego to solve a current life problem, which appears as the focal conflict of the dream. For example, a male patient who was married and the father of three children reported dreaming that he "was mixing cement." While free associating to the dream, he mentioned that his house needed some repair work done on its external walls. French and Fromm say this very brief dream expresses an effort to solve a key emotional problem in the man's life—how to take better care of his family, how to "hold their house together." However, the dream shows the strategy he is using to solve this problem is inadequate: "Instead of interacting with his wife and children directly, he 'mixes (lifeless) cement'" (1992, 185).

As this example indicates, dreams reveal not only what the focal conflict is, but also how the dreamer is trying to solve it. French and Fromm believe that dreams have great value as illustrations of a person's basic cognitive structure and the ego's favorite defensive and integrative strategies to use in dealing with waking-life problems.

In the case of long and elaborate dreams, the focal conflict is brought into relation with analogous conflicts and problems the dreamer has faced in the past. A person who is having troubles with a supervisor at work might dream of past conflicts with authorities like parents, priests, teachers, and so on; the dream would bring up these memories in order to help the ego see what worked and what didn't work when facing similar problems earlier in life. These memories from the past constitute the dream's historical background, and French and Fromm insist that a better understanding of this background can provide valuable assistance in the dreamer's efforts to solve the focal conflict.

People often wonder why dreams contain such a hodgepodge of characters and settings. A dream might take us back to an early school classroom, but with decorations from a hotel in a different country, and with people whom we saw yesterday at the local grocery store. What possible meaning could a dream have with such disparate, jumbled elements? French and Fromm argue that the seemingly garbled content of people's dreams *always* has a meaning. Dreams will bring up anything—any memory, image, or experience—that might be relevant to the ego's need to solve the current focal conflict. Stated differently, this means every element in the dream, no matter how random or bizarre, is connected to the focal conflict.

This makes interpreting dreams difficult, French and Fromm admit, because the same dream may show the focal conflict being denied, being addressed in a childish fashion, being compared to other current life problems, and being maturely and creatively resolved, all at the same time. Thus, they recommend that interpreters try using a variety of approaches and, most importantly, rely on their empathetic imaginations to guide them. French and Fromm compare interpreting a dream to interpreting a work of art, in that the first step of the process should be allowing one's intuition and imagination to scan the dream. By listening carefully for little hints of significance, and by moving back and forth between the dream as a whole and its various parts, the analyst will gradually formulate an interpretive hypothesis about the dream's overall meaning. French and Fromm explain that "the interpretive hypothesis is correct if it illuminates or explains every bit of the dream text plus every single association given to it as part of a *total response the dreamer has made to his actual current emotional situations*" (194, emphasis in original). Failure in dream interpretation comes from unwillingness to follow one's intuitions, from getting "side-tracked on a Sub-Focal Conflict," (194) and from becoming prematurely fixated on one hypothesis about a dream's meaning. There are two tests to use in judging an interpretive hypothesis: the scientific one of critically checking the dream and associations for any inconsistencies with the hypothesis and the aesthetic one of feeling pleasure at the beautiful whole of the dream, a sense of recognizing the dream in its totality, "usually with a joyful 'Aha!' experience" (188).

Ultimately, French and Fromm believe the goals of dream interpretation are to identify the focal conflict, to clarify the cognitive structure the dreamer is using to solve that conflict, and thereby to facilitate better waking-life functioning.

Gestalt Psychology: Frederick Perls

Frederick Perls was a German medical doctor who combined Freudian psychoanalysis, existentialism, and Gestalt psychology into an innovative and highly influential approach to dream therapy. Perls did his basic psychoanalytic training in Germany, but when the Nazis came to power in the 1930s, he left the country and immigrated to South Africa. While working there, he studied the growing body of psychological research on the Gestalt aspects of cognitive functioning. (*Gestalt* is a German word meaning form, pattern, or shape.) This research suggested that human perception is a matter of instantly grasping complex and interrelated patterns. We do not initially perceive two legs, two arms, curly hair, freckles, a big smile, and then conclude, "That's my friend Tom." Rather, we initially perceive the total Gestalt of Tom, the overall pattern that can later be broken down into separate perceptual elements like legs, hair, smile, and so forth. Perls expanded Gestalt psychology's concepts to psychotherapeutic practice, helping people to learn to recognize and expand the Gestalt of their own individual personalities. He agreed with leaders of the Humanistic Psychology movement like Abraham Maslow and Carl Rogers that psychoanalytic and behaviorist models of psychology only speak about the absence of pain and unhappiness—they say nothing positive about what a healthy, fulfilling life is like. In his writings and especially in his therapy groups (conducted most famously at the Esalen Institute in Big Sur, California, in the 1960s), Perls developed an approach to dreams that aimed to promote not just the cure of neurosis, but also the experience of creative, healthy living.

Perls says, "All impoverishment of the personality comes about by self-alienation—by disowning parts of ourselves" (1970b, 212). All psychological illness is caused by holes in the Gestalt of an individual's personality. To cure illness and enhance genuine health, the disowned parts must be reclaimed and reintegrated into the personality Gestalt. Dreams, according to Perls, are one of the best means of learning where the holes in an individual's personality lie. "Freud once called the dream 'the royal road to the unconscious,'" Perls says, "[but] I believe that it is really the royal road to *integration*" (1970b, 204).

Perls regards dreams as spontaneous creations of the dreamer's own mind. As such, every element of a dream reflects some element of the dreamer. Nothing in a dream is coincidental; nothing is meaningless. Every aspect of a dream "is a part of the dreamer, but a part that to some extent is disowned and projected onto other objects" (1970a, 27). Although this sounds similar to Jung's notion of the subjective level of interpretation (see chapter 3), Perls is actually making a quite different claim about the nature of dreaming. He does not speak of dreams as tapping into deep archetypal undercurrents flowing in and through each individual psyche; rather, Perls considers dreaming as the direct product of the individual self, "an existential message . . . of yourself to yourself" (1970a, 27).

The therapeutic approach that Perls takes toward dreams is guided by the basic existential principle of trying to help the dreamer re-experience the dream in the waking state as immediately, as intensely, and as fully as possible. Because each element in the dream reflects some disowned part of the individual's personality, the individual can begin to reintegrate those parts by identifying with each aspect of the dream. Perls disdains any kind of dream analysis that distracts the dreamer from the feelings and sensations experienced in the dream. He insists on people describing their dreams in the present tense, not the past, and encourages them to imagine *being* each element of a given dream. Below is a sample dialogue from one of Perls's dream seminars. A woman ("C.") has described a dream in which she sees a lake that is drying up, with some porpoises on an island, and an old license plate on the bottom of the lake:

> Perls: *Will you please play this license plate.*
> C.: I am an old license plate, thrown in the bottom of a lake. I have no use because I'm of no value. I'm not rusted, I'm outdated. So, I can't be used. I'm just thrown on the rubbish heap. That's what I did with the license plate—I threw it in the rubbish heap.
> Perls: *Well, what do you feel about the dream?*
> C.: I don't like it. I don't like being an old license plate—useless.
> Perls: *Could you talk about it until you come to be the license plate.*
> C.: Useless—outdated. The use of the license plate is to allow—to give a car permission to go—and I can't give anyone permission to do anything because I'm outdated. In California they just paste a little—you buy a sticker and stick it on the car—on the old license plates. So, maybe someone would put me on their car and stick a new sticker on me. I don't . . .
> Perls: *O.K. Play now the lake.*

> C.: I am a lake. I am drying up and disappearing—soaking into the earth—*dying*. But, when I soak into the earth and become part of the earth maybe, I water the surrounding area, so—even the lake—even in my bed—flowers can grow. New life can grow from me—[C. is starting to cry]
>
> Perls: *Do you get the existential message?*
>
> C.: Yes, I can—I can create. I can create beauty. . . . [As] the water and the lake, I can play a part. (1970b, 213–214)

As this dialogue indicates, Perls encourages his clients to identify with and play the role of every element in their dreams: feeling what it is like to *be* that element, looking at the rest of the dream from its unique perspective, and reflecting on how that element has been expressed, or disowned, in the Gestalt of the dreamer's personality.

Perls also guides his clients in exploring areas of tension between elements in the dream that oppose or conflict with each other. He gives particular attention to instances of what he calls the "topdog vs. underdog" opposition. "Topdog" is the demanding voice of our ideals, trying to control our behavior, forcing us to be good; "underdog" is the unsteady voice of our resentments, unable to fight topdog directly but determined to resist its righteous demands. Perls believes that many dreams express topdog versus underdog "games" within the dreamer's personality. For example, if someone dreamed of an angry adult trying to punish a disobedient child, Perls would have the dreamer identify first with the adult and then with the child, back and forth, letting the two opposing dream characters dialogue and really "have it out." In this way, the dreamer would be able to experience both the topdog adult and the underdog child as aspects of him- or herself. Perls would try to help the dreamer move from having a conflict between the adult and child to *being both*, and thus to integrating them.

While admitting that this process is not easy, Perls says, "If we work long enough, then you come through to an understanding and . . . an appreciation of differences" (1970b, 212). Successful Gestalt dream therapy enables people to stop projecting disowned parts of themselves out onto the world and to begin taking full responsibility for all aspects of their personality. With a total acceptance of one's actual self and a commitment to living in the "here and now," Perls believes that people will finally be able to "*wake up* and become real. . . . The task of all deep religions, especially Zen Buddhism, or of good therapy, is the Great Awakening—the coming *to one's senses*—waking up from one's dream, especially from one's nightmare" (1970b, 215, emphasis in original).

The Cognitive Experiential Method: Clara Hill

Psychotherapeutic practices began to change toward the end of the 20th century for at least two reasons. First, a new generation of psychoactive medications became available that provided many people with significant relief from a variety of mental illnesses. This meant that fewer patients were seeking psychotherapy for problems that could now be resolved with the use of the proper drugs. Second, clinicians (and the insurance companies who have increasingly become their primary sources of payment) began questioning the evidence that Freudian, Jungian, or any other kind of therapy actually *works* in terms of improving people's lives. Instead of long-term analysis involving an open-ended exploration of the client's past, clinicians began looking for short-term methods focused on making tangible improvements in the client's ability to deal with specific problems in the present.

In many ways, this new approach revives the principles of Alfred Adler, discussed earlier in this chapter. Adler advocated for exactly this kind of practical attitude toward correcting unhealthy or maladaptive patterns of behavior. His ideas influenced Albert Ellis and Aaron T. Beck, who went on to develop "Cognitive Behavioral Therapy" (CBT). The CBT approach, combined with the use of psychoactive medications, has become the most widely used treatment regime in the mental health system of the early 21st century.

The rise of the drugs-and-CBT approach has corresponded with a sharp decline in the use of dreams in psychotherapy. While many people benefit enormously from drug treatments, the side effects of several medications frequently have a negative impact on dreaming, with disrupted REM sleep, increased nightmares, and decreased dream recall (see Pagel 2010). Practitioners of CBT typically have little time or patience for working with dreams, given the importance of speed and measurable effectiveness in their treatments.

In response to this drift away from the clinical use of dreams, Clara Hill of the University of Maryland has led a resurgence of attention to dreaming as a valuable resource in treating people with various kinds of mental health problems. She and her colleagues have shown that dreams have a proven effectiveness in short-term therapy, much more so than generally assumed by those who practice in the CBT world. Starting with her 1996 book, *Working with Dreams in Psychotherapy*, she has developed a simple but powerful method for drawing useful material from dreams in a CBT context.

Hill's approach to dream interpretation involves three stages: *exploration, insight,* and *action*. The exploration stage seeks to highlight the "cognitive schema" of the dream by asking the client a series of questions about the images, feelings, and associations from the dream. The insight stage centers on a process of constructing a personal sense of meaning from the dream. Hill acknowledges that several possible dimensions of meaning can emerge at this point, including reflections of waking concerns, parts of the self, early childhood conflicts, and existential or spiritual concerns. "An important point in constructing a meaning of the dream is to let the client know that there is no one correct meaning of the dream, but the interpretation should seem to the client like a good 'fit'" (Spangler and Hill 2016, 125). In the action stage, the therapist and client talk about how to use the meanings of the dream to make changes in waking life. To spur the discussion, the therapist can ask the client what he or she would change in the dream and then shift the conversation toward ways of translating those changes into specific areas of thought and behavior in waking life.

Hill's 2004 edited book, *Dream Work in Therapy*, made good on one of the chief goals of her model, namely to create an approach to dream interpretation in therapy that can be measured in terms of its effectiveness, so she can identify what exactly makes it so valuable. She and several of her colleagues described the applications of her method with various kinds of clients, and they used standard methods of measuring therapeutic effectiveness to evaluate the results. They found that clients enjoy working with their dreams in this way and consider the process a good source of insight. It gave the clients a more favorable attitude toward making changes in their lives, and it helped decrease the symptoms of depression and increased feelings of well-being. Further research has supported the claim that dream-sharing practices facilitate personal insight (Edwards et al. 2013).

In Milton Kramer's edited book, *Dream Research* (2016), Hill co-authored a chapter with Patricia Spangler titled "The Hill Cognitive-Experiential Model: An Integrative Approach to Working with Dreams." It highlights the finding from several research studies that "clients thought that the most valuable components of the model were cathartic release, new insights, and links to waking life" (Spangler and Hill 2016, 127).

The three stages of the Cognitive-Experiential Method can be performed within a single session of therapy, making it possible to include dreams even in very short-term treatment. Hill's approach can also be extended to long-term therapies and integrated with other theoretical viewpoints. But her emphasis from the start has been to provide psychotherapists from all backgrounds with a simple and reliable set of interpretive principles that can be employed in virtually any mode of treating mental illness and also beneficially applied to the dreams of mentally healthy people, too:

> I present this model as a self-contained therapeutic intervention, or thera-peutic module or mini-therapy. In other words, a person comes to therapy with a dream that he or she wants to understand, and a therapist works with him or her to understand the dream. This intervention can take place in one or two sessions for a relatively healthy person whose goal is primar-ily self-discovery or growth. The model can also be used in single sessions or within the course of brief or long-term therapy. (2004, 11)

Alternative Clinical Answers to the Three Basic Questions

Formation

On the question of how dreams are formed, the five theories discussed in this chapter all see a fundamental continuity between dreaming and waking experience. Adler, Boss, and Perls all reject the notion (shared by Freud and Jung) that dreams originate far away in the depths of the unconscious; they insist that dreams are shaped by the same personality structures that operate while we are awake. These include Adler's "style of life," Boss's "being-in-the-world," and Perls's "spontaneous creativity." French and Fromm, while retaining many elements of Freud's dream the-ory, also put greater emphasis on the connection of dreaming and waking patterns of personality (what they call a dream's "cognitive structure"). Hill devotes less attention to issues of dream formation, but she agrees with French and Fromm that both dreaming and waking experiences are built upon a shared cognitive foundation.

Function

Adler is alone among the five in minimizing the positive, constructive, and creative functions of dreaming. Like Freud, Adler sees dreams as self-deceptions that are useful only in diagnosing weaknesses and failings in the personality. Boss, French and Fromm, Perls, and Hill also believe that dreams provide valuable diagnostic insights into the dreamer's current psychological condition, but they go on to argue that dreams can bring forth new creative energies that lead beyond the ordinary capacities of the dreamer's waking consciousness. Perls calls dreams "the royal road to integration" for their capacity to help people reclaim parts of themselves they have disowned. French and Fromm see dreams as elaborate and often very creative efforts to solve a focal problem in the dreamer's life. Boss says that the extraordinary freedom people experience while dreaming enables the discovery of truly transcendental aspects of human existence. Hill and her colleagues have found that a cognitive-experiential approach can open people to unusually vivid and impactful insights about spiritual or existential concerns.

Interpretation

All five theories speak against rigid, simplistic methods of dream interpretation, and they insist that any interpretation must be grounded in the realities of the dreamer's life. Adler's approach puts special emphasis on the emotions felt during a dream, taking them as significant clues to discovering the dreamer's style of life. French and Fromm regard dream interpretation as akin to the interpretation of art, in the need to follow the guidance of one's intuition and empathetic imagination. The theories of Adler, French and Fromm, and Hill are close to Freud's in relying heavily on the dreamer's free associations and in seeking a comprehensive explanation of every detail of a given dream. Boss and Perls, however, depart sharply from Freud. Boss dismisses free association, amplification, and anything else that leads the dreamer away from the immediate felt experience of the dream; he asks not what a dream symbolizes, but what mode of being-in-the-world the dreamer experiences in the dream. Similarly, Perls rejects the overly intellectual cast of Freudian interpretation and encourages the dreamer to identify with each element of the dream, as an element of the dreamer's own self. Hill also brackets out the digressive complexities of Freudian and Jungian interpretation and encourages the dreamer to attend very closely to the dream at hand, focusing on its experiential realism and its immediate, practical relevance for waking life.

Sleep Laboratories, REM Sleep, and Dreaming

I had been dreaming about getting ready to take some kind of exam. It had been a very short dream. That's just about all that it contained. I don't think I was worried about it.

I was dreaming about exams. In the early part of the dream, I was dreaming that I had just finished taking an exam and it was a very sunny day outside. I was walking with a boy who was in some of my classes with me. There was a sort of a . . . a break, and someone mentioned a grade they had gotten in a social science exam, and I asked them if the social science marks had come in. They said yes. I didn't get mine because I had been away for a day.

> —Two dreams, the first from NREM sleep and the second
> from REM sleep, reported by the same subject on
> the same night (Dement, 1972, 44)

In the first chapter of *The Interpretation of Dreams*, Freud gave a detailed survey of the findings of 19th-century experimental dream researchers. These researchers had devoted careful study to the possible connections between the mental content of dreams and the physical conditions of a dreamer's sleeping body. They had found, for example, that certain forms of external stimulus would frequently enter into a person's dream. If the researcher rang a bell near the ear of a sleeping person, the sound might appear in the person's dream as an alarm clock or a fire engine or a church bell. Similarly, the researchers found that certain internal stimuli would also enter into people's dreams. Being feverish might lead to a dream of walking through a hot desert; having a full bladder might produce a dream of watering flowers in a garden.

But after reviewing the work of these investigators, Freud essentially dismissed their findings as unimportant. He argued that such experiments, while interesting, really tell us nothing fundamental about the formation or functions of dreaming. Why, he asked, does one person hear the stimulus of a ringing bell and dream of an alarm clock, while another person hearing the exact same stimulus dreams of a church bell? Why do some people fail to incorporate external stimuli like ringing bells into their dreams, and why do other people dream of alarm clocks and church bells without hearing any external stimuli? Because experimental researchers had failed to provide good answers to these questions, Freud decided their work could not contribute anything of real value to the modern psychology of dreaming. He concluded, "What we are concerned with is not the origin of certain special dreams, but the source that instigates the ordinary dreams of normal people" (1965a, 69).

Most psychologists following Freud agreed with this negative conclusion about the value of experimental studies of dreaming. For the next five decades, the primary focus of dream research was on the clinical work of psychotherapists. Because they have direct access to the intimate personal lives of their clients, psychotherapists seemed to have the ideal background to answer basic questions about the nature of dreams.

But soon a serious problem arose with this exclusively clinical approach to dream psychology. Every clinician seemed to come up with a different theory about the nature of dreaming. Alternative models, methods, and approaches multiplied rapidly. Rather than moving toward greater clarity and consensus, dream psychologists appeared to be moving further and further apart, with their theories increasingly contradicting one another.

A dramatic change in the history of 20th-century dream psychology occurred in the 1950s when sleep laboratory researchers discovered the phenomenon of *rapid eye movement (REM) sleep* and its associations with dreaming. Suddenly the possibility opened up that dreaming could be objectively observed, precisely measured, and experimentally studied in a controlled laboratory situation. At long last, it appeared a truly scientific psychology of dreaming could be developed.

This chapter will describe the original research on REM sleep and will discuss how the subsequent explosion of laboratory investigations of REM sleep has transformed the modern psychology of dreaming.

Aserinsky and Kleitman's Discovery of REM Sleep

Nathaniel Kleitman was a physiologist at the University of Chicago who had spent many years studying the nature of sleep, particularly the effects of sleep deprivation. One of his students was Eugene Aserinsky, who was doing graduate work investigating aspects of attention in children. While collecting data for his project, Aserinsky noticed one day that the children's eyes began shifting around very quickly beneath their lids whenever they lost attention and fell asleep. These darting eye movements were completely different from the slow, rolling eye movements that researchers had long observed occurring at sleep onset. Aserinsky mentioned his observations to Kleitman, and when they began more careful study of the children, they were surprised to find that these eye movements were very much like a person's eye movements while awake. Aserinsky and Kleitman conducted further experiments, and they soon learned that these periods of highly intensified eye movements, which occurred in both children and adults, were accompanied by distinctive brain wave patterns, irregular breathing, and increased heart rates.

The results of their research were as clear as they were revolutionary. They found that the brain does not simply turn off when a person goes to sleep, resting peacefully until it is turned back on in the morning. Aserinsky and Kleitman had found that at regular points during the night our brains become very active—indeed, sometimes more active than when we are awake. William Dement, a medical student who became a member of Kleitman's research team, coined the term "rapid eye movement sleep," or REM sleep, to designate this newly discovered brain state. About Aserinsky and Kleitman's discovery, Dement later wrote,

> This was *the* breakthrough—the discovery that changed the course of sleep research from a relatively pedestrian inquiry into an intensely exciting endeavor pursued with great determination in laboratories and clinics all over the world. . . . For the first time we realized what has probably been true of man's sleep since he crawled out of the primordial slime. Man has *two* kinds of sleep. His nocturnal solitude contains two entirely different phenomena. (1972, 25)

Aserinsky and Kleitman published their initial findings in 1953 in the journal *Science*. They published a longer article in 1955, titled "Two Types of Ocular Motility Occurring in Sleep," in the *Journal of Applied Physiology*. Their 1955 article discussed the possibility that REM sleep is associated with dreaming. They reported that subjects who were awakened after a period of REM sleep gave detailed dream accounts 20 out of 27 times; subjects who were awakened after a period of NREM (non-rapid eye movement) sleep gave dream accounts only 4 out of 23 times. Aserinsky and Kleitman concluded, "The evidence for the association of the rapid eye movements with dreaming, or at least the recall of dreaming, is strong" (1955, 8–9). They found that some of the dream reports following REM periods involved "strikingly vivid visual imagery," leading them to suggest that "it is indeed highly probable that rapid eye movements are directly associated with visual imagery in dreaming" (1955, 9).

Early Research on REM and NREM Sleep

The first sleep laboratory studies following Aserinsky and Kleitman's original work concentrated on mapping out more carefully these new features of the terrain of sleep. Researchers soon determined that a typical night's sleep for an adult human follows a regular alternation of REM sleep and four stages of NREM sleep. Sleeping individuals are said to "descend" through the four NREM stages in that their sleep becomes deeper, they become more remote from the external environment, and stronger stimuli are required to wake them up.

As shown in figure 5.1, when people fall asleep they descend from stage 1 NREM to stage 2 and then stage 3, and finally stage 4. (In recent years, researchers have decided to collapse stages 3 and 4, so there are only three total stages of NREM sleep.) After being asleep for an hour or so, people will start moving "up" through the NREM stages until, approximately 90 minutes after sleep onset, the first REM period of the night begins. Brain wave activity increases dramatically, muscle tone diminishes, heartbeat and respiration become irregular, and blood flow to the genitals increases (resulting in enlargement of the clitoris in women and erection of the penis in men). This first REM period lasts for ten minutes

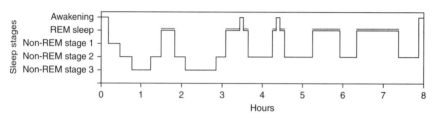

Figure 5.1

or so, and then the sleeping person descends again through the NREM stages to the "deepest" levels of stages 3/4, before rising up to the next REM period. Throughout the night this cyclical alternation between NREM and REM sleep continues, with an average of 90 minutes between the onset of one REM period and the next. As the night goes on, the REM periods increase in duration, and by the end of the night, they may last as long as an hour. Conversely, the NREM periods become shorter. Stages 1, 3, and 4 more or less disappear, and the sleeper alternates almost exclusively between stage 2 NREM sleep and REM until awakening. On average, then, adult humans experience four or five periods of REM sleep each night, which amounts to approximately one-quarter of their total sleep time.

Research by Dement and Michel Jouvet, a French neurosurgeon, demonstrated that a very similar cycle of REM-NREM sleep alteration occurs in cats (Jouvet 1999). Other sleep laboratory researchers soon confirmed that nearly all mammals experience substantial amounts of REM sleep (see McNamara 2004 and Horne 2007). Most reptiles appear to have NREM sleep but nothing like REM sleep. Birds, according to Dement, "have very well developed NREM sleep, and show occasional, very brief (one second) episodes of what appears to be an evolutionary precursor of the REM period" (1970, 30).

Researchers also found that for many mammals the percentage of REM sleep is higher among newborns than among adults (Roffwarg et al. 1966). Newborn kittens, puppies, rats, and hamsters, for instance, have nothing but REM sleep. For human infants, at least half of their sleep is REM, and REM periods have been detected in the sleep of human fetuses. Sleep laboratory researchers have taken all of this as strong evidence that REM sleep serves some evolutionary function in the activation and maturation of the brains of young mammals.

As researchers tried to understand the nature and possible functions of REM sleep, they conducted deprivation experiments to see what would happen if people were prevented from having any REM sleep at all. In these experiments, subjects were allowed to sleep through the NREM stages but were awakened every time they entered REM sleep. Dement conducted one of the first deprivation experiments, and he reported that his subjects became anxious, irritable, and unable to concentrate after five days of REM deprivation. He speculated, "If the dream suppression were carried on long enough, a serious disruption of the personality would result" (1960, 1707).

However, later experiments by Dement and others did not confirm the suggestion that depriving people of REM would cause terrible psychological damage. What these experiments did demonstrate, though, was a "rebound effect": a REM-deprived subject will, when allowed to sleep again through a night without interruption, experience a dramatic increase in REM sleep. Following a period of REM deprivation, a subject will in subsequent nights enter REM sleep more quickly and stay in it longer. Researchers have taken this as indicative of a strong physiological need for REM sleep. Interestingly, researchers have also conducted experiments depriving subjects of NREM sleep and have found similar rebound effects. It seems that mammals need both REM sleep *and* NREM sleep.

Another set of sleep laboratory experiments on both humans and animals looked at the relationship of REM sleep to learning and information processing. For example, animals who underwent difficult learning tasks were found to have increased amounts of REM sleep the following nights. Likewise, humans who were faced with complex or stressful learning tasks experienced higher percentages of REM sleep. When their REM sleep was disrupted or entirely eliminated, both animals and humans were less able to retain new information (see Smith 1993 and Maquet, Smith, and Stickgold 2003). Some researchers focused specifically on REM sleep and the processing of information with a high emotional charge. Ramon Greenberg and his colleagues conducted an experiment in which subjects were shown a stressful movie (a graphic portrayal of an autopsy). Half of the subjects were then REM-deprived the night following the movie, and half were awakened during NREM periods. When shown the movie a second time, the REM-deprived subjects reacted with markedly more anxiety than did the other subjects. Without the benefits of REM sleep, these subjects were evidently less able to manage the stress of a repeat viewing of the movie. Greenberg and his colleagues concluded that REM sleep seems to function in helping us to emotionally process anxiety-provoking situations and experiences (Greenberg et al. 1972). However, later researchers have questioned the sleep-learning connection, suggesting the relationship is more complex than initially assumed (Vertes and Eastman 2003; Rasch and Born 2013).

Another important research project, conducted by Rosalind Cartwright and her colleagues, focused on investigating the dream characteristics of people going through a major life change (women going through a divorce). She found that among the women who were not significantly depressed by their divorce, REM dreams were longer, portrayed a wider range of events through time, dealt with negative emotions, and portrayed the dreamer's self in marital roles. By contrast, among the women who were depressed by their divorce, REM dreams were less visual and story-like, had a narrower and more past-oriented time frame, did not identify the dreamer with any marital roles, and generally avoided any mention of the divorce. When Cartwright did follow-up interviews with the depressed women, she found that as their waking moods improved their dream characteristics changed in the direction of the non-depressed women. She concluded that dreams definitely do respond to major events in waking life and that "when affect levels in response to events are moderate, dream changes appear to be more adaptive than when events are accompanied by disruptively high affect levels" (Cartwright et al. 1984, 259).

The changes to modern psychological knowledge produced by the discovery of REM sleep cannot be overestimated. In the space of just a few years, sleep laboratory researchers demonstrated that while we sleep our brains engage in a cyclical pattern of highly complex activities. These activities frequently become so intense that they are indistinguishable from the brain's activities while we are awake. Neuroscientist J. Allan Hobson, whose work will be discussed later in this chapter, has said that if sleep researchers could only look at the measurements of the electroencephalogram (EEG) machines that measure brain wave patterns, they would have difficulty distinguishing the brain state associated with waking from the brain state associated with REM sleep. "If we were not able to observe that a subject is behaviorally awake in the first case and sleeping in the second, the EEG alone would not be capable of indicating whether a subject is awake or [in REM sleep]" (1988, 136).

REM, NREM, and Dreaming

The crucial question remains: what exactly does REM sleep have to do with dreaming? As noted above, Aserinsky and Kleitman's 1955 article argued there is strong evidence that REM sleep and dreaming are associated. Kleitman and Dement published two articles in 1957 that indicated that subjects awakened immediately following a REM period reported dreams far more frequently than did subjects awakened during NREM sleep. Their findings gave rise to the belief that REM sleep and dreaming are identical, or *isomorphic*—we dream when we are in REM sleep, and we don't dream when we are in NREM sleep. Some researchers began to refer to REM as "dreaming sleep."

But other researchers questioned this hasty assumption of REM-dreaming isomorphism. David Foulkes, who did his doctoral work in the University of Chicago's sleep laboratory, challenged the idea that NREM sleep is a dreamless void by raising the crucial issue of how researchers were defining the phenomenon of "dreaming." When Foulkes awakened his subjects from NREM sleep, he asked them, "Was anything going through your mind?" rather than, "Were you dreaming?" He found that more than 50 percent of the time subjects reported mental occurrences from NREM sleep with visual, auditory, and/or physical sensations (Foulkes 1962). Foulkes said the NREM reports tended to be shorter, with less intense visual imagery, physical activity, and emotional involvement than dream reports from REM sleep. However, he argued that many of the NREM mental occurrences could still plausibly be regarded as dreams; at the very least, they are legitimate phenomena of sleep and deserve study as such.

Other researchers confirmed Foulkes's findings. The two dreams quoted at the beginning of this chapter indicate the general differences many studies found between the mental activities of NREM and REM sleep. In his book *Some Must Watch While Some Must Sleep* (1972) Dement concludes,

> Compared with REM recall, NREM mentation is generally more poorly recalled, more like thinking and less like dreaming, less vivid, less visual, more conceptual, under greater volitional control, more plausible, more concerned with contemporary lives, occurring in lighter sleep, less emotional, and more pleasant. The impression is that NREM mentation resembles that large portion of our waking thought that wanders in a seemingly disorganized, drifting, nondirected fashion whenever we are not attending to external stimuli. (44)

But even this broad generalization that NREM reports are more thought-like and REM reports are more dream-like has been challenged by later research. While very vivid and elaborate dream narratives are rarely found during NREM, many NREM reports cannot be distinguished from REM reports. The differences, Foulkes has said, are distributional rather than categorical: the dream-like qualities of emotional intensity, visual vividness, physical activity, and so forth occur on average more frequently in REM reports than in NREM reports. But many REM reports do not possess such qualities, while many NREM reports do (Kahan 2001, 2003) (see also Nielsen 2003).

The exact relationship between REM sleep, NREM sleep, and dreaming continues to be studied and debated by researchers. But almost all scholars in the field agree on at least these points:

• REM sleep is not identical to dreaming.
• NREM sleep is not a dreamless void.
• Mental activities occur through all stages of the sleep cycle.

Based on all the studies researchers have performed since Aserinsky and Kleitman's breakthrough discovery, it seems certain that REM sleep has some special connection to dreaming. However, it remains unclear what precisely this connection may be.

Hobson's Activation-Synthesis Hypothesis

A highly influential effort to specify the connections between REM sleep and dreaming has been made by neuroscientist J. Allan Hobson. First in a 1977 article, "The Brain as a Dream-State Generator: An Activation-Synthesis Hypothesis of the Dream Process" (co-authored with Robert W. McCarley), and then in his 1988 book *The Dreaming Brain*, Hobson sets out to demonstrate that the neurological activity of the brain during REM sleep creates both the sense and the nonsense of dreaming. Hobson has written several other books and articles about dreams, but he establishes the basic framework of his approach in these two initial writings.

From the opening pages of *The Dreaming Brain* it is clear that Hobson is writing directly against Freud and the psychoanalytic theory of dreams. But Hobson is attacking not only Freud, for he sees psychoanalysis as the culmination of a long history of dream interpretation, which he calls "the prophetic tradition." According to this tradition, dreams are caused by external beings, contain secret coded messages, and require elaborate interpretations by special authorities. In Hobson's view, psychoanalysis is but the latest version of this ancient approach, with Freud claiming that dreams come from the mysterious unconscious, bearing deviously disguised wish fulfillments that cannot be understood without the aid of a skilled psychoanalyst. Hobson claims that psychoanalysis has changed the language, but the essentially superstitious perspective remains the same.

Rather than obeying the dogmas of this prophetic tradition, stretching from the Bible to Freud, Hobson says he will follow the tradition of science, "in which experimental accomplices or instrumentation have been used to make the study of dreams more systematic and more objective" (1988, 12). His approach is to provide a scientific explanation for how dreams are formed. With that explanation as a basis, he will be able to show what dreams mean.

Drawing on modern neurological research, Hobson says that a constant competition between groups of neurons in the brain leads to the cycles of waking, sleeping, and dreaming:

> REM sleep and dreaming are the result of a temporary domination of one neuronal population over another. Victorious is a troop of reticular-formation neurons concentrated mainly in the pontine portion of the brain stem; owing

to their fusillades of firing in association with REM-sleep events, these pontine reticular neurons are likely to play the executive role in the generation of REM sleep and dreaming. Sharing the white flag of temporary surrender is a population of aminergic neurons . . . ; hardly a shot is fired by this neuronal phalanx during REM sleep. (183)

The key conclusion Hobson draws from this model, which he calls the "reciprocal-interaction model of REM-sleep generation," is that REM sleep is caused by neurological processes that are involuntary, cyclical, and rooted in our physiological nature.

To account for how the activity in neuronal populations in the brain during REM sleep is transformed into the psychological experience of dreaming, Hobson offers the "activation-synthesis hypothesis of dreaming." This hypothesis suggests that after neuronal processes have activated REM sleep, higher brain functions work to synthesize the essentially random input as well as it can, with dreams being the result. Hobson says, "The activation-synthesis hypothesis assumes that dreams are as meaningful as they can be under the adverse working conditions of the brain in REM sleep. The activated brain-mind does its best to attribute meaning to the internally generated signals" (214). In the synthesis stage of dream formation, the mind makes sense of the nonsensical, random neurological activity, creating meanings where there were none before.

Although Hobson admits that we still know far too little about how the synthesis process actually works, he claims his activation-synthesis hypothesis can account for the most important formal features of dreaming. For example, his hypothesis explains the predominantly visual character of dreams as the result of certain neuronal processes of REM sleep that stimulate visual receptors in the brain, leading the mind to think it is seeing external objects, characters, and settings. Likewise, Hobson's hypothesis explains the strong emotional content of many dreams as the product of emotional systems in the brain that become randomly activated during REM sleep, spontaneously making us feel angry or sad or excited; our mind responds to these sudden emotional upsurges by weaving together images and stories that try to make sense of the feelings. The distortions that are so common in dreams occur because the mind simply cannot make any real coherence or meaning out of the random, bizarre data that is continuously generated by the brain during REM sleep. Hobson and McCarley say in their 1977 paper, "Such features as scene shifts, time compression, personal condensations, splitting, and symbol formation may be directly isomorphic with the state of the nervous system during dreaming sleep. In other words, the forebrain may be making the best of a bad job in producing even partially coherent dream imagery from the relatively noisy signals sent up to it from the brain stem" (1977, 1347).

The role of synthesis in dream formation reveals, Hobson believes, an essentially human capacity to imagine and create. His theory "sees the brain as so inexorably bent upon the quest for meaning that it attributes and even creates meaning when there is little or none to be found in the data it is asked to process" (1988, 15). Hobson says the brain labors, in sleeping and waking, to create a meaningful integration of its experience, "even if it must resort to creative storytelling" (219). Indeed, the utterly chaotic neural firings that bombard us in REM sleep often confound all ordinary means of organizing our perceptions, leading to extraordinary attempts at synthesis. Hobson grants that perhaps the "symbolic, prophetic character [of dreams] arises from the integrative strain of this synthetic effort. The brain-mind may need to call upon its deepest myths to find a narrative frame that can contain all the data" (214).

A crucial consequence Hobson draws from the activation-synthesis hypothesis is that the meaning of dreams is not hidden or coded, but rather is clear, obvious, and present right on the surface of the dream: "For activation-synthesis the dream as reported is the transparent and directly legible product of an unusual mode of information processing" (217). Whatever meaning there is to a dream, it comes during the process of synthesis, with no masks or deceptions. Dreams have their origins in purely random neural activity, and this proves, Hobson claims, that the prophetic tradition's demand for complex interpretations by authoritative specialists is groundless.

Hobson presents his own dreams and the dreams of "The Engine Man" (a middle-aged scientist who, in 1939, carefully recorded 233 of his dreams in a journal) as evidence to show that the meanings of dreams are in fact clear, undistorted, and readily understood. With his own dreams, Hobson finds that his feelings, wishes, perceptions, and thoughts are all easily recognized; "this all seems very transparent to me. Almost naked" (233). Activation-synthesis can account for many of the strange features of his dreams, and his own common sense can explain the rest.

The Dreaming Brain ends with a discussion of the basic functions of REM sleep. Hobson says that REM sleep helps the brain maintain its basic neural circuits. Our regular daily activities do not draw on all our brain's potential abilities, so REM sleep works to exercise the brain, regularly activating all its neural circuitry in the physically safe environment of sleep. (The only neural systems not activated during REM sleep are those responsible for critical attention in waking life, because these systems are very sensitive and easily exhausted.) Hobson likens our brain to a car sitting in a garage—we need to "rev our cerebral motor" at least once a day so that it stays in good working condition.

Hobson claims that once the neurological basis of REM sleep is properly understood, it becomes clear that dreams are simply the mind's creative attempts at making sense of the random neural activities of the brain. Dreams do not come from spirits, gods, or even the dark wishes of the unconscious; dreams come from the brain, and they highlight the fundamentally artistic nature of human beings, with intense determination to make meaning, even where none really exists. While he agrees with Freud that dreams may be interpreted for personal meanings, Hobson says his position "echoes Jung's notion of dreams as transparently meaningful." He continues:

> I wish again to emphasize strongly that I am not asserting that dreams are either meaningless or unworthy of clinical attention. On the contrary . . . the meaning of dreams is for me transparent rather than concealed, since fundamentally incoherent cognitive elements are synthesized in a personally meaningful way. This "meaning-added" process is the exact opposite of that envisaged by psychoanalysis, which asserts that fully coherent and deeply meaningful ideas (the latent dream content) must be degraded and disguised (by the dream-work), resulting in an incoherent product (the manifest content) acceptable to consciousness. For me, the manifest content is the dream: there is no other dream. (12, 258)

In more recent work, Hobson and his colleagues have expanded the scope of his theory to do a better job of accounting for dream experiences (such as lucidity and self-awareness within dreaming) that have more high-level cognitive activities than the original activation-synthesis hypothesis would allow. In his new model, Hobson explains the whole wake-sleep-dream cycle in terms of three variables: **a**ctivation, **i**nformation source, and **m**ode, which yields the acronym AIM. *Activation* represents the electrical output of the brain, usually measured by the EEG. The *information source* is either external, as in waking, or internal, as in sleep and dreaming. The *mode* refers to the balance of neurotransmitters governing the brain, which Hobson defines as either the aminergic system (dominant in waking) or the cholinergic system (more active in REM sleep).

In the terms of this model, waking can be defined as state of high activation drawing on external information and controlled by the aminergic neurotransmitters. NREM sleep is defined as a state of low activation, internal information, and neither aminergic nor cholinergic neurotransmitters in charge. And REM sleep is defined as a state of high activation, internal information, and cholinergic control. The AIM model explains lucid dreaming as a state of REM sleep in which the mode of neurotrans-mitters shifts just enough to allow for some conscious thought to enter the dream process.

These considerations have led Hobson to a slightly more favorable view of the possible functions of dreaming. He notes, "The motor programs in the brain are never more active than during REM sleep . . . [in order] to prevent their decay from disuse, to rehearse for their future actions when called on during waking, and to embed themselves in a rich matrix of meaning" (Hobson 1999, 117). He is even willing to agree that Freud was correct about the basic idea that "dreams are trying to tell us something important about our instincts (sex, aggression), our feelings (fear, anger, affection), and our lives (places, persons, times)" (90).

Mark Solms, Neuropsychology, and Brain Imaging

Approaches like Hobson's, which emphasize a unidirectional, bottom-up influence of brainstem processes on dream formation, have been challenged by Mark Solms and his neuropsychological research on the dreams of people with various kinds of brain damage. Neuropsychology is the discipline that focuses on the treatment of brain pathologies and their negative impact on mental life. Solms studied the sleep and dream patterns of 361 patients in a South African hospital over several years, and he made a careful analysis of the correlations between different kinds of brain damage and dreaming symptoms. Most of the patients suffered no problems with their dreams. These people had damage to parts of the brain responsible for waking thought, awareness, and eyesight, but they continued to dream just as they had before the damage occurred. This suggests the dream formation system in the brain has a fair degree of durability and resilience—it can keep functioning even if major portions of neural territory have been compromised.

Solms created four groups to describe the symptoms of the patients who did report changes in dreaming: *global anoneira*, a total loss of dreaming; *visual anoneira*, limited or non-existent visual dream imagery; *anonei-rognosis*, increased frequency and vivacity of dreaming; and *recurrent nightmares*, an increase in the frequency and intensity of emotionally disturbing dreams. The correlations between these symptoms and damage to specific regions of the brain led Solms to formulate several hypotheses about dream formation. First, there are many brain regions contributing to dream formation, not just one single generating center. This means dreaming is a widely distributed and non-modular process similar to other complex mental faculties. Second, a total loss of dreaming can occur after damage to either one of the cerebral hemispheres of the brain. This indicates that normal dreaming requires bilateral arousal, drawing on networks spanning both sides of the brain. Third, Solms found a "double dissociation" between visual imagery in dreaming and visual perception while awake. People whose brains were damaged in areas of the brain involved in eyesight could not see while waking, but still had normal vision in dreams, and people whose brains were damaged in neural areas devoted to internal imagery and visual association lost their vision in dreams, but still could see normally in waking life. The implication of this remarkable finding is that visual experience has different neural foundations in waking and dreaming. What we see in waking life is processed by a different part of the brain from what we see in dreaming.

The fourth and most important hypothesis to come from Solms's neuropsychology research is that the essential neural systems required for dreaming do *not* include the brainstem's activation in REM sleep. Solms argues, "The neural mechanisms that produce REM are neither necessary nor sufficient for the conscious experience of dreaming" (Solms 1997, 153). Instead, his findings indicate that several areas of the brain (e.g., basal forebrain pathways, medial occipito-temporal structures, the inferior parietal region, the frontal-limbic region, and temporal limbic structures) are crucial for dreaming, all of which also support conscious mental functioning in the waking state. Solms refers to these brain regions as connected to "some of the highest regulatory and inhibitory mechanisms of the mind" (153). Although Solms takes no interest in the interpretation of dreams, his work supports a recognition of dreaming as a remarkably complex mental activity with deep roots in the basic operations of the human brain.

In addition to neuropsychological studies like Solms's, further developments have come from the use of sophisticated tools for scanning brain activities, including functional magnetic resonance imaging (fMRI), positron emission tomography (PET), and single-photon emission computed tomography (SPECT). These technologies can give detailed images of activation levels in various parts of the brain, although they currently require the subjects to remain almost perfectly still and motionless during the measurement process. This limits the use of brain scanning devices for the study of sleep and dreams, since the natural state of sleeping involves a fair amount of physical movement during the course of cycling from NREM to REM sleep and back again. However, researchers have successfully managed to apply these tools with sleeping people, and the results are very encouraging (see Braun et al. 1997; Nofzinger et al. 1997; and Maquet, Smith, and Stickgold 2003).

The pattern of regional activation from waking into NREM sleep and then into REM sleep seems to follow these contours, most of which corresponds closely with Solms's findings using a different methodological approach. According to research using various kinds of brain scanning devices, the *occipito-temporal region* is central for sensory perception in waking, and it diminishes in NREM sleep then reactivates in REM sleep. This part of the brain seems to support visual, auditory, and other sensory experiences in dreaming. The *limbic system*, which underlies our emotions and instinctual responses in waking, becomes highly aroused in REM sleep, accounting for the prominence of these features in dreaming. Many regions of the prefrontal cortex are relatively deactivated in REM sleep; these parts of the brain are associated with short-term memory and selective attention, which do seem less prominent in dream content. An exception to lower prefrontal activity is a rise in arousal from the medial prefrontal cortex, a brain region that contributes to social intelligence and "theory of mind" reasoning about other people's subjective thoughts, feelings, and intentions. The high frequency of characters and social interactions in dreams makes sense in light of the active contribution of this part of the brain (see Dang-Vu et al. 2007).

Research using these tools of brain analysis has many limitations, so such findings should be treated cautiously. But future discoveries are bound to accelerate in coming years as the technologies become more sophisticated and more finely tuned in their measurements. The challenge for investigators will be to recognize both the common patterns in neural functioning across all members of our species *and* the unique qualities of psychological experience, development, and potential for each individual human.

Crick and Mitchison's Reverse Learning Theory

In 1983, an article titled "The Function of Dream Sleep" was published in the journal *Nature* by Francis Crick, the Nobel Prize-winning co-discoverer of the DNA molecule, and Graeme Mitchison, a neuroscientist at the Salk Institute in La Jolla, California. Based upon their research into the workings of the mammalian cerebral cortex, Crick and Mitchison offer in this article a new explanation for the function of REM sleep and an alternative view of the nature of dreaming. They start with Hobson's notion of REM sleep as a means of maintaining good cerebral functioning, but they take it in a quite different direction. Crick and Mitchison argue that rather than just giving the brain's neural circuitry a little exercise each night, REM sleep focuses specifically on eliminating potentially damaging patterns of brain activity.

Crick and Mitchison begin their argument with the observation that the brain's network of interconnected cells is so complex and sensitive that "unwanted or 'parasitic' modes of behavior" can easily take hold when it is disturbed either by the brain's natural growth or by external experience (111). To perform as well as it does, the mammalian brain must have some way to rid itself of these negative neural patterns, and Crick and Mitchison claim that REM sleep serves this function: "We propose that such modes are detected and suppressed by a special mechanism which operates during REM sleep and has the character of an active process which is, loosely speaking, the opposite of learning. We call this 'reverse learning' or 'unlearning'" (111).

Although Crick and Mitchison admit their reverse-learning theory is quite speculative and extremely difficult to test, they insist that it makes sense of two basic facts from sleep laboratory research: REM sleep is especially prominent in infancy, and almost all of our dreams are, in ordinary circumstances, forgotten. Infants need so much REM sleep because their brains are developing at a rapid rate, and many faulty or improper neural connections are accidentally being made. REM sleep helps in the necessary process of cleaning out those faulty connections, allowing the more useful ones to be strengthened and built up. We still need REM sleep in adulthood because even mature brains occasionally suffer from the development of parasitic modes of neural activation, requiring the regular use of the neural self-cleaning process. Regarding the fact that most of our dreams are forgotten, Crick and Mitchison say this occurs for the simple reason that dreams are *meant* to be forgotten—the focus of dreaming in REM sleep is on precisely those neural patterns that the brain needs to eliminate. Crick and Mitchison go on to suggest that the practice of dream interpretation may inadvertently reverse the function of REM sleep: "In this model, attempting to remember one's dreams should perhaps not be encouraged, because such remembering may help retain patterns of thought which are better forgotten. These are the very patterns the organism was attempting to damp down" (114).

The "Lab Effect"

Throughout the history of sleep laboratory investigations of dreaming, researchers have debated the question of how much influence the laboratory setting itself has on the subject's dreams. When people sleep in a laboratory, they typically lie down in a strange bed and have electronic wires attached to their head, torso, and sometimes even genitals. They know that other people are going to be watching them all night long, and they know they will suddenly be awakened a number of times during the night and asked by strangers to answer a series of questions. It is only natural that the experience of sleeping in a setting like this will trigger anxiety in many of the people who serve as research subjects. This anxious awareness will thus filter into their dreams. For example, research subjects frequently have dreams that incorporate explicit features of the laboratory setting—the wires, bed, room, lab assistants, and so on. Many of their dreams also include indirect but unmistakable references to the lab setting, such as dreams of being tested or talking to a doctor or being paid to do a difficult job.

As part of a 1962 sleep laboratory study by R. Whitman and his colleagues at a veteran's hospital in Cincinnati, Ohio, the researchers tried to ease the subjects' fears by showing them around the lab, carefully explaining what the EEG machine does, and answering all their questions about the project. However, Whitman concluded that, despite these efforts to make the subjects more comfortable, the lab effect on their dreams remained strong:

> It is clear in this study that neither reassurance about the [laboratory] apparatus nor repeated episodes of exposure to the apparatus were sufficient to decrease anxiety about the experimental situation, even over a period of four weeks. Surface cooperativeness and surface placidity may well hide massive fears and anxiety reactions which would affect physiological, biochemical, and, of course, psychological measurements. (Whitman et al. 439)

A few years later, Calvin Hall and Robert Van de Castle (whose work will be described in more detail in the next chapter) compared dreams reported in a sleep lab with dreams reported in a home setting. They found the home dreams had more aggression, friendliness, sex, misfortune, and good fortune; overall, the home dreams seemed to have a greater "dramatic quality" than did the lab dreams (Van de Castle 1994, 284). Hall commented on these findings, "Although there is no way of knowing at the present time what 'typical dream life' is like, it is a plausible assumption that it will not be found in a laboratory setting no matter how normal the environment provided to the subject" (1967, 206). In Van de Castle's book *Our Dreaming Mind* (1994), he notes that nocturnal emissions, or "wet dreams," are extremely rare among subjects who are sleeping in a laboratory setting, which he takes as further evidence that the lab has an inhibiting effect on people's dreams (237).

Ernest Hartmann's research on nightmares (also to be discussed in the next chapter) gives still another perspective on the power of the lab effect.

He found that "nightmares almost never occur spontaneously in the sleep laboratory in normal subjects, and even persons who report frequent nightmares at home have much fewer in the laboratory" (1984, 37). Hartmann suggests that when people sleep in a lab they feel a sense of protection, a sense that the trained staff will prevent any harm from coming to them during the night.

Taken together, these research findings indicate that the sleep laboratory has the effect of homogenizing people's dreams—making it less likely that people will experience, remember, and/or report their unusual, emotionally intense dreams. Certain types of dreams (such as highly sexual or aggressive dreams, nightmares, and perhaps other extraordinary modes of dreaming) seem to elude capture by the machinery of the sleep lab. This means that studies relying on laboratory data alone may not give a truly accurate and comprehensive picture of the human dreaming experience.

Nevertheless, other researchers have argued that the lab effect can be minimized and that the sleep laboratory remains the best tool available for investigating the nature of dreaming. Research by Dement, for example, has shown that after their first night in the lab, subjects usually incorporate fewer elements from the experimental situation into their dreams (Dement et al. 1965). As a consequence, almost all sleep labs now allow their subjects to sleep through the first night of the experiment without any interruptions, to give people a chance to get more comfortable with the lab setting.

David Foulkes argues vigorously that proper research methods can eliminate all negative influences due to the lab effect, and he goes on to assert that the sleep laboratory is an indispensable device for investigating dreams. In his research on children's dreams Foulkes insists that only dream reports gathered in a laboratory are sufficiently representative for the purposes of scientific study. He rejects investigations based on spontaneously remembered dreams from home settings because "the sampling bias [is] horrendous" (1982, 175). The multiple factors influencing both the quantity and quality of children's dreams recalled at home are so unpredictable that no legitimate conclusions can be drawn from them.

> What conclusions about the workings of the child's mind in sleep, or about individual differences in these workings, could possibly be based on nonrandom, incomplete sampling of this kind? The dream student's choice cannot be dreams which are reported "truly spontaneously"; the only reasonable question facing such a student is where and how to study dreams deliberately and systematically. . . . [S]ince the undoubted gains in

representative sampling in the laboratory are in no significant way jeopardized by losses in the representativeness of the dreams being sampled, the most reasonable answer to this question is: "in the laboratory." (136)

As with so many issues in modern dream psychology, the nature and significance of the "lab effect" continues to be debated.

The Sleep Laboratory's Answers to the Three Basic Questions

Formation

Sleep laboratory researchers have found that almost all mammals experience the regular and cyclic occurrence of rapid eye movement (REM) sleep, when the brain becomes highly active, heart rate and respiration increase, and the eyes jerkily dart about underneath the lids. The typical sleeping pattern for humans involves the alternation between REM and several stages of NREM sleep. On average, adult humans spend about a quarter of their sleep time in REM; newborn humans (and the newborns of many mammals) experience a far higher percentage of REM sleep. After being deprived of REM sleep, people experience a rebound effect in which they have more REM sleep on the nights following the deprivation. REM sleep seems to play a role in the learning of new information and the processing of emotionally significant events from daily life. Sleep laboratory researchers do not, however, agree on how closely REM sleep should be identified with dreaming. This makes it difficult to derive from their work any clear, definite answers to the three basic questions about dreaming. At present, it appears that dreams reported from REM sleep tend to be more vivid, emotional, and active than dreams reported from the various stages of NREM sleep. Thus, it seems that dreaming is to a significant degree generated and shaped by the complex neural activities of the brain during REM sleep. And because all humans experience REM sleep, laboratory research indicates that all humans dream every single night, whether or not they remember having dreamed when they wake up.

Function

On the question of dream function, sleep laboratory researchers have suggested that dreaming may promote the early growth and adaptation of the brain; may help people respond effectively to novel, complex, or anxiety-provoking experiences; and may generally work to process new information learned during the day. The fact that almost all mammals experience REM sleep, while reptiles and fish do not, indicates that dreaming may have some evolutionary value.

Interpretation

Few sleep laboratory researchers devote sustained attention to the question of how to interpret dreams. Hobson makes the most noteworthy effort to correlate scientific knowledge about REM sleep with methods of interpreting the meanings of particular dreams, although his claims about REM-dreaming isomorphism have been contradicted by the findings of Solms and other neuroscientists.

Cognitive Psychology and Dreaming

> Mummy made a big, green statue out of leaves. A fox came and knocked it over by pushing its head into the leaves. I was frightened of the fox and went back into Mummy's inside to hide. Then he couldn't catch me.
>
> —Five-year-old girl (Piaget 1962, 178)

Cognitive psychology involves the systematic study of the mind and its information-processing capacities. Its primary subjects are the nature and development of perception, language, reason, memory, and imagination. Many cognitive psychologists have taken an interest in dreaming, investigating it as a possible source of evidence regarding the basic structures and workings of the mind. How is dreaming like, and unlike, waking consciousness? What special mental operations are involved in constructing the experiences that occur in sleep? How are the images and settings of dreams formed? Where does the spoken dialogue come from? Which parts of a dream come from old memories, and which parts (if any) are freshly created? How are people and objects from waking life represented in dreaming? How are the dreams of adults related to the dreams of children? Does a capacity for dreaming develop in tandem with the general cognitive development of a maturing human?

In recent years, a great deal of high-quality research on the cognitive psychology of dreaming has been published. Because no single chapter could adequately cover all the available material, this chapter concentrates on the more limited task of profiling the pioneering researchers in this area, outlining their major projects, and describing their responses to the dream theorists who preceded them. The common theme in the work of these researchers is that dreaming is a product of the human mind and should thus be studied using the same systematic methods used to investigate other forms of mental functioning. In the view of these researchers, clinicians from Freud onward have failed to use adequate scientific methodologies in their investigations of dreams. And even if sleep laboratory researchers have performed genuinely scientific experiments, they have focused almost exclusively on the nature of REM sleep rather than on dreaming per se. The aim of cognitive psychologists has been to fill this void by performing focused empirical studies on how and why the human mind creates dreams.

Jean Piaget on Play, Dreams, and Imitation in Childhood

By all accounts, Swiss psychologist Jean Piaget is one of the great figures of modern cognitive psychology. Originally trained in biology, Piaget turned early in his career to the study of psychology, specifically the development of human intelligence. His goal was to integrate the theoretical speculations of philosophers and psychoanalysts with empirical data gained from careful scientific research. Over the next several decades, Piaget produced a considerable number of books and articles examining many different facets of cognitive development.

Drawing on his background in biology, Piaget defined intelligence as an organism's ability to adapt to its environment—meaning that human language, reason, and imagination can be understood and analyzed as special tools for helping us adapt successfully to the world in which we live. He argued the intellectual growth of children should be a primary subject of psychological research because in children we find the evolutionary origins of all forms of mature adult cognitive functioning.

Piaget's chief study of children's dreams is *Play, Dreams, and Imitation in Childhood*, originally published in 1946. In this book, he examines how children learn to adapt to the world around them. Piaget says their efforts follow two basic strategies: *accommodation* and *assimilation*. The purest form of accommodation is imitation, when children try to repeat exactly what they have seen or experienced; through imitation, they try to accommodate themselves to the demands of objective reality. The purest form of assimilation is play, when children create and control their own imaginary worlds; through play, they try to assimilate objective reality to the demands of their subjective wishes and desires. By means of these two strategies of accommodation and assimilation, children can gradually develop a realistic view of the external world, a strong individual ego, and a balanced, well-adjusted relationship between objective and subjective realities.

Piaget regards children's dreaming as a continuation of the kind of symbolic play that is common between the ages of three and five, and he identifies a number of similarities between the two phenomena. First, both dreaming and playing express children's basic physical and emotional desires, and they create imaginary fulfillments of those desires. Second, both can take a painful experience from the child's life and give it a different and happier ending. Third, both dreaming and play use simple forms of primary symbolism, which refer more or less directly to conscious thoughts (such as daily events and experiences). And fourth, both can use more complex forms of secondary symbolism, which refer to deeply unconscious wishes and feelings (for instance, relating to the child's body, emotions toward family members, and anxieties about childbirth). Piaget considers the five-year-old girl's dream quoted at the beginning of the chapter to be an excellent example of how children use secondary symbolism to express unconscious desires. He says of the girl,

> [She] had asked shortly before [having the dream] how a statue of greenish bronze had been made, and she was also afraid that the foxes in the neighborhood might kill the animals she was rearing. But whatever the assimilations may be which would explain these images, the fact remains that [the girl], when frightened by the fox coming to destroy the statue, felt in her dream that the safest thing for her to do was to return to her mother's womb. (1962, 181)

According to Piaget, the occurrence of nightmares reveals the only real difference between children's playing and dreaming. Fears and anxieties are commonly expressed in both playing and dreaming, "but in play there is always more or less conscious control, while in dreams control is more difficult, because the situation is assimilated to more deeply-seated schemas, i.e., to a more remote past" (180).

Piaget rejects Freud's theory that dreams are intentionally disguised by a censoring mechanism within the mind. Instead, he aligns himself with Jung's view that the symbolic images of dreams reflect basic mental patterns and structures common to all humans. Although Piaget disagrees with Jung's claim that certain symbolic contents are inherited (and thus he agrees with Freud that the capacity for symbolism originates anew in each individual), he does say we should accept Jung's important notion that there is a level of primitive symbolic thought in each person's mind.

However, to explain the origins and operation of this level of thought, Piaget argues that,

> We must come back to the child's visible and analyzable psycho-genetic development. We are indebted to Freud for confining the problem of unconscious symbolism to the level of individual evolution. Once the idea of disguise is removed, symbolism can, thanks to the truly primitive character of the mechanisms of the child's thought, acquire the same degree of generality that Jung found in his hypothesis of a "collective unconscious." (198)

The ultimate goal of cognitive development, Piaget says, is to reach an equilibrium between the two strategies of accommodation and assimilation, a point of balance he calls "intelligent adaptation" (86). Healthy development requires that the distorted, egocentric fantasies of playing and dreaming become integrated with the individual's perceptions of and experiences with objective reality. When this occurs, playing and dreaming are transformed into the power of "creative imagination," a power that stimulates the further growth of human intelligence in adulthood.

Calvin Hall, G. William Domhoff, and Content Analysis

Calvin Hall was an American psychologist whose prolific dream research began in the 1940s and continued until his death in 1985. He developed a means of studying dreams, the content analysis method, that has become one of the most influential and widely practiced techniques for the scientific study of dreams. Hall presented his research and theories in three major books: *The Meaning of Dreams*, first published in 1953 and revised in 1966; *The Content Analysis of Dreams*, co-authored with Robert Van de Castle in 1966; and *The Individual and His Dreams*, co-authored with Vernon Nordby in 1972.

The human fascination with dreams has led to many attempts to explain them, Hall says. The origin of dreams, for example, "has been attributed to such diverse sources as the absence of bed covers or the presence of spirits" (Hall and Van de Castle 1966, ix). Hall grants that Freud's dream theory went a long way toward providing a rational explanation of dreams, but since Freud's time, little real progress has been made: "It is true that others have advanced different theoretical interpretations of what constitutes the hidden message within dreams, but the methodology of investigating dreams has remained fixed at a qualitative stage of development" (Hall and Van de Castle 1966, ix).

Hall tries to advance the scientific study of dreams by inventing a quantitative method of content analysis. This method involves taking a written dream report and sorting its content into various structural elements. (The five major categories Hall uses are characters, social interactions, emotions, settings, and objects.) These elements are identified, tabulated, and then converted into numbers and statistically compared to large bodies of data gained from other dream reports. With this method, researchers are able to minimize the influence of subjective biases and develop conclusions that are solid, easily replicable, and clearly communicable to other researchers.

A 21-year-old male college student, who was unmarried and worked part-time as a Fuller Brush salesman, reported the following dream:

> I was in a classroom teaching young women several things about cosmetics, hair care, etc. I remember getting into a big discussion on the virtues of natural hair brushes vs. nylon ones and the correct way to brush hair. The class was about 30 women about age 18 in a classroom much like we had in high school (fixed desks, and old building). The women all paid attention and discussed things well. (Domhoff 1996, 267–268)

According to the Hall and Van de Castle system, this dream would be coded as follows. The characters in the dream are the dreamer and a group of adult females unfamiliar to the dreamer. The seven objects are the classroom and the old building (coded as two architectural objects of a vocational nature), the cosmetics, natural hair brushes, nylon brushes, and desks (coded as four household objects), and the hair (coded as a part of the body, specifically the head). The dream's setting is indoors, in a place of uncertain familiarity to the dreamer. The only social interaction is a friendly one, with the dreamer teaching the women about personal grooming. The only activity in the dream is a mutual verbal discussion between the dreamer and the group of women. There are no measurable emotions (anger, fear, happiness, sadness, or confusion) in this dream (Domhoff 1996, 268–269).

Once a dream like this is coded by the Hall and Van de Castle system, it can be quantitatively compared to a series of other dreams reported by the same individual. Examining a long series of dreams enables researchers to determine such facts as the average number of objects in the individual's dreams, the frequency of indoor versus outdoor settings, the presence or absence of certain emotions, the emotional quality of male-female interactions, and so forth. And when the dream scores of large groups of people are gathered and analyzed, researchers can quantitatively examine the differences in dream content between children and adults, between men and women, and between various social and ethnic groups.

Hall acknowledges that the content analysis method does not ask for personal associations from the dreamer, which Freud, Jung, and many other psychologists insist is necessary for any legitimate study of dream content. But Hall replies that dream reports have great psychological significance apart from the personal associations of the dreamer, and he disputes Freud's distinction between the manifest and latent contents of dreams:

> It could be said that there is no such thing as the latent content of a dream. A dream is a manifest experience, and what is latent lies outside the dream and in the verbal material that the dreamer reports when he is asked to free associate to features of the reported dream. How the psychoanalyst arrives at the "true meaning" or interpretation of the dream from the verbalized associations is more of an art than a technique. This art may be of the utmost value in the therapeutic situation, but being a private, subjective type of activity it is of no direct value for research. (Hall and Van de Castle 1966, 20)

Personal associations may be helpful for the interpretation of dreams in clinical psychotherapy, but in Hall's view, they add nothing to objective scientific research on dreams.

Based on his content analysis method, Hall develops a theory that dreams are essentially projections of the mind that represent the subjective reality of the dreamer. He expands on Freud's fundamental claim that dreams reveal our unconscious instinctual impulses. Hall says dreams do more than tell us that a person has sexual and aggressive impulses: "They tell us what a person *thinks* about these basic impulses, what people they are directed against, and how they can best be satisfied" (Hall 1966, 70). For Hall, the symbols that appear in dreams are a kind of mental shorthand that help to express the person's thoughts (and not hide them, as Freud taught):

> Dreaming is a form of thinking and thinking consists of formulating conceptions or ideas. When one dreams, his conceptions are turned into pictures. The images of a dream are the concrete embodiments of the dreamer's thoughts; these images give visible expression to that which is invisible, namely, conceptions. Accordingly the true referent of any dream symbol is not an object or activity, it is always an idea in the mind of the dreamer. (1966, 95–96)

In *The Individual and His Dreams* Hall says that content analysis has demonstrated a simple truth about dreams. There is a close correspondence between people's dreams and their concerns in waking life. He calls this the "continuity hypothesis" of dreams, which asserts, "The world of dreaming and the world of waking are one" (Hall and Nordby 1972, 104). People generally dream about the same people with whom they have the closest relationships in waking life. The wishes and fears that appear in dreams are the same as those that guide waking thought and behavior. Hall says that while a few dreams obviously deviate from waking life, content analysis has proven that people's dreams tend to be continuous with their concerns, interests, and beliefs while awake.

An interesting finding of Hall's research regards differences in dream content among men and women. He and other investigators using the content analysis method have found that women's dreams on average include more indoor settings, more friendly interactions, and more characters who are familiar to the dreamer. Men's dreams, meanwhile, on average contain more outdoor settings, more aggression, and more characters who are strangers to the dreamer. Most significantly, Hall found that in men's dreams almost two-thirds of the characters are males, and only one-third are females; by contrast, women's dreams contain an equal number of male and female figures. Hall termed this a "ubiquitous sex difference" because dozens of research studies on many different groups of subjects have replicated this sizable disparity in the percentage of male and female characters in men's and women's dreams (Hall and Domhoff 1963a). Researchers are still investigating whether this gender difference in dream content is a product of differences in male and female biology or cultural differences in how boys and girls are educated or some combination of the two (Van de Castle 1994, 318–328).

Although its primary aim is to increase scientific knowledge about the workings of the human mind, the content analysis method does offer a means of personal dream interpretation. The key, Hall says, is always to analyze a *series* of dreams, because this makes it quite easy to identify the larger patterns of meaning that are woven through each individual dream. (Recall that Jung made a similar point about the importance of dream series.) With this approach to dream interpretation, no special theoretical knowledge or technical skills are required:

> The dreams read like chapters in a book. When put together in order as we have done there is organization, unity, and coherence among the dreams. Each dream complements or supplements the other dreams of the series. There is very little left to guesswork since what may seem ambiguous or

hidden in one dream is revealed in another dream. Dream interpretation based upon a series of dreams can be very precise and objective if one approaches the task in a scientific manner. (Hall 1966, 84–85)

Among the many important research studies that have been performed using the Hall and Van de Castle system, one deserves special mention. G. William Domhoff, who was one of Hall's closest colleagues, has written a sweeping summary of content analysis research on dreams titled *Finding Meaning in Dreams: A Quantitative Approach* (1996). In the concluding chapter of this book, Domhoff examines what he calls the "repetition dimension" in dreams. By studying recurrent dreams; the nightmares of trauma victims; the widespread "typical" dreams of flying, falling, and so on; and the repeated elements in long series of dreams from one individual, Domhoff finds that repetition is a major feature all across the spectrum of dream content. He says that the repetition dimension is further evidence for Hall's continuity hypothesis, showing that people generally dream about the ongoing personal concerns and interests of their lives and that people's dreams are surprisingly similar to their waking-life thoughts and feelings. Domhoff argues, "No theory of dreams [should] be taken seriously if it cannot deal with the repetition dimension we show to be very prominent in dreams and dream content" (1996, 186).

More recently, Domhoff has elaborated a neurocognitive theory of dreaming that aligns studies of dream content with current research on the "default network" of brain functioning (Raichle and Schneider 2007; Fox et al. 2013; Domhoff 2011a). The default network represents the mind's activities when it is not engaged in a task requiring focused mental attention. It is, in other words, a state of mind wandering, and its neurological profile corresponds very closely with brain activation patterns in sleep. This promising thesis has the potential to integrate research findings at many levels of scientific analysis.

Recent developments in computer technology have allowed for the analysis of dream content to improve in both speed and precision. Domhoff and his colleague Adam Schneider have built the DreamBank website (dreambank.net) as a resource for studying large collections of dreams and analyzing them using elements of the Hall and Van de Castle coding system. Domhoff's 2003 book, *The Scientific Study of Dreams: Neural Networks, Cognitive Development, and Content Analysis*, showed how to combine these new analytic technologies with research in the cognitive functions of dreaming. Inspired by the DreamBank resource, in 2009 I created the Sleep and Dream Database (SDDb), an online, searchable archive devoted to empirical dream research. The SDDb includes dream journals, demographic surveys, and historical reports that can be explored using various methods of text analysis. The DreamBank, the SDDb, and other digital resources offer powerful new opportunities for studying patterns in large collections of dreams.

David Foulkes on Dreaming and Language

As mentioned in the previous chapter, David Foulkes was originally trained in the sleep laboratory at the University of Chicago, where he performed important research on the relations between REM and NREM sleep. But Foulkes gradually became convinced that physiological studies of REM and NREM sleep could not answer key questions about how the mind forms dreams. He decided that the best hope of answering these questions would come from using the latest models and methodologies of cognitive psychology, especially the recent findings that cognitive psychologists have made about the development of language. In three major books—*A Grammar of Dreams* (1978b), *Children's Dreams: Longitudinal Studies* (1982), and *Dreaming: A Cognitive-Psychological Analysis* (1985)—as well as in dozens of articles, Foulkes has argued that modern dream psychology must work to bring its research efforts more fully into the mainstream of cognitive psychology.

Foulkes's stance toward the psychological study of dreams is well stated in this passage from the first chapter of *A Grammar of Dreams*:

> One major obstacle to a full-fledged acceptance of dreaming as thinking is our reluctance to take responsibility for our dreams. Among many lay people and students of psychology this reluctance often takes the form of a belief in the supernatural (e.g., religious, telepathic) determination of dream content. For those who think of themselves as scientists, however, there always has been a degree of commitment to the working hypothesis that dreams, like all other mental phenomena, must be explained in terms of the natural minds of the persons who experience them. . . . [U]nless we are to take the "miracle" hypothesis literally, unless, that is, we are going to accept some supernatural explanation of dreams, we *must* be assigned sole responsibility even for the most "delicate" of our dream scenarios. It can be no other way. We appropriately may stand in awe of the generativity of the sleeping mind which creates such dreams. But we must go beyond awe to understanding. (1978b, 3–4)

Foulkes not only insists that dreaming can be exhaustively explained as a product of the "natural powers of the mind," he argues that dreaming is generated by the same cognitive systems that produce ordinary speech in waking life. Dreams do not speak in a "special language"; they speak in the same basic language, following the same basic grammatical rules, that we use when we are awake.

The study on children's dreams that Foulkes conducted over a five-year period at the University of Wyoming demonstrated both the ordinariness of dreaming and its dependence on general cognitive and linguistic development. The study involved two groups of children (one starting at ages 3–4, the other starting at ages 9–10) who slept in the laboratory for nine non-consecutive nights every other year. A total of 46 children participated, and Foulkes made 2,711 awakenings during the five years. His basic findings were that children's dreams become longer, more active, and more complex as children grow up. The three- to five-year-olds in his study recalled the fewest dreams, and the dreams that they did report were very short and static. Usually these younger children did not appear as characters in their own dreams, or they appeared only as passive observers. Animal figures were remarkably common in these children's dreams. The reports of the five- to six-year-olds gradually became more "dreamlike" in terms of action, theme, and narrative complexity. The seven- to eight-year-olds had dreams with still greater degrees of dynamism and symbolic sophistication. By early adolescence the dreams were regularly including characters and themes from the broader social world (school, peer groups, etc.) and had become comparable to adult dreams in terms of length and structure.

Foulkes concludes that, contrary to popular stereotypes, children's dreams are not filled with overwhelming anxieties, simple wish fulfillments, or profound archetypal symbolism. Rather, children's dreams are quite ordinary expressions of how their developing minds are processing daily life experiences: "The most common plot sequences in the child's dream involve everyday forms of social interaction, with a particularly strong emphasis on play activity. Plot resolutions in dreams tend to be realistic and appropriate, rather than grandiosely self-serving" (1979, 148). Children's dreams are thus powerful evidence that dreaming is a cognitive process that develops in complexity, sophistication, and power along with other cognitive processes.

In his studies of adult dreaming, Foulkes challenges another common belief: dream are not wild, random, utterly bizarre creations, but are in fact quite orderly, coherent, and well structured. Dream reports gathered from people sleeping in the laboratory indicate that the vast majority of dreams obey the same basic rules of logical association that govern our waking thought and language. While Foulkes grants that dreams do emerge out of personally relevant thoughts and emotions, he sees no proof that dreams are saying anything in particular. Unlike waking speech, dreams are not intended to communicate a specific message: "I conclude that we have no sense of intention during dreaming and we are unable, asleep or awake, to reconstruct plausibly why we dreamed a particular dream because there was no intention in the formation of any particular dream image" (Foulkes 1982b, 176–177). For Foulkes, as for Freud, the essence of dreaming is a set of cognitive mechanisms by which thought and language are structured: "That is, mechanisms whose investment is not so much in saying any particular thing as in insuring that whatever is said is literally and thematically comprehensible" (1982b, 186).

Foulkes's key argument is that the sleeping mind is not functionally distinct from the waking mind. The human mind is always operating as an information-processing system, whether it is producing waking thoughts during the day or dreams during the night.

Although he is skeptical about any effort to interpret special meanings hidden in dream contents, Foulkes affirms that dreaming probably does serve a number of valuable psychological functions:

- The complex stories and plots found in dreams suggest that dreaming allows people to exercise their powers of narrative integration, making symbolic knowledge more easily accessible to waking consciousness: "Becoming human is, from this perspective, learning to understand and to be able to tell 'stories.' Dreaming surely might play some role in this process" (1985, 202).

- The complex forms of sensory imagery created by the dreaming mind indicates that dreaming helps promote "the multimodal representation and integration of symbolic knowledge" (1985, 202).

- The appearance in dreams of memories from the recent past and from the distant past makes it likely that dreaming contributes to our conscious ability to retrieve and integrate various kinds of memory.

- The strange, "unreal" quality of dreaming "permits an enhancement of the range of 'world' experiences to which our minds are exposed. On the one hand, this could help to program our minds to deal with novel situations adaptively. On the other hand, the very unreality of dreams could contribute to the development of what Freud called 'reality testing'" (1985, 203).

- The various forms of conscious thought and self-reflection experienced while dreaming "may contribute to the development and elaboration of a distinctively human self-consciousness. What we know about dreaming in early childhood is at least consistent with this possibility" (1985, 203).

Harry Hunt and the Multiplicity of Dreams

Foulkes's strictly grammatical and anti-intentional approach to the cognitive psychology of dreams has generated a number of spirited rebuttals. The most sophisticated of these responses to Foulkes comes from Harry Hunt, a psychologist at Brock University in St. Catharines, Ontario.

In *The Multiplicity of Dreams* (1989), Hunt argues that cognitive psychology must draw upon the observations and findings of other academic fields (e.g., anthropology, history of religions, literary criticism) if it wants to develop a truly comprehensive model of dream formation and function. While Foulkes insists that only dream reports gathered from the sleep laboratory are valid evidence, Hunt replies that the more unusual types of dreams reported outside the sleep lab can offer special insights into the potentialities of the dreaming process. He says, "Laboratory dreams are generally fairly boring, while it is precisely the more infrequent variations that call attention to dreams in the first place and make them uniquely worthy of study" (92). Dreams must be studied in their natural setting if we are to understand their true characteristics and functions.

After examining the full spectrum of different dream types, the common *and* the rare, Hunt offers the following classification:

- *Personal-mnemonic dreams*: relating to ordinary, daily matters in the dreamer's personal life
- *Medical-somatic dreams*: relating to physiological processes in the dreamer's body; frequently occur during an illness or following an accident
- *Prophetic dreams*: presenting omens or images of the future that may come true
- *Archetypal-spiritual dreams*: involving vivid, powerful encounters with seemingly transcendent forces; sometimes include extremely strong physical or "titanic" sensations
- *Nightmares*: filled with terrifying and deeply upsetting images, themes, and emotions
- *Lucid dreams*: involving consciousness within the dream that the individual is dreaming

Hunt says these different types of dreams do not occur with equal frequency. On the contrary, some of them occur very rarely. But it is vitally important, he says, that we recognize the genuine existence of *all* these types:

We find in each historical era and phase of culture a shift in relative importance across a common spectrum of dream typologies. But despite these shifts in the predominant definition and theory of dreaming, despite the contrasting ontological assumptions of these cultures, there is evidence that the same forms of dream experience continue to recur. . . . [T]here is a natural order of dream forms. (90)

Hunt challenges all dream theories that are based solely on the characteristics of only one of these dream forms. (For instance, he says that Foulkes and Freud considered only dreams of the personal-mnemonic type in developing their theories.) Hunt's goal is to develop a cognitive psychological understanding that can account for the processes that generate *all* the different types of dreams, giving us "insight into a deeper unity of dream formation" (74).

The chief task, as Hunt sees it, is to reconcile two opposing approaches to the question of how dreams are formed. According to one general theory, held by Foulkes, Freud, Hobson, and several cognitive psychologists, dreaming involves a battle between the forces of mental chaos and mental order. The partly random, partly organized imagery of our dreams results from an uneasy compromise between these two warring forces. The research focus here is on the constructive activities of the forces of mental order: how exactly are the chaotic images and memories thrown up by the unconscious during REM sleep cognitively transformed into the partially organized products of our dreams? Freud describes the four mechanisms of the dream-work, Hobson speaks of the "synthesis" side of activation-synthesis, and Foulkes refers to the grammatical structures governing ordinary speech. In each of these theories, dreams are explained as the products of higher-level mental processes that impose order on the disruptive lower-level neural inputs.

Hunt says the other general approach to dream formation, best expressed by Jung and by James Hillman (a prominent Jungian analyst), asserts that the seemingly disruptive forces in dreams are actually the spontaneous expressions of a powerful symbolic intelligence that is different from but not inferior to waking rational thought. Here, the research focus is on the incredibly bizarre and fantastic images that fill many dreams. What can waking consciousness learn from these mysteriously creative dream images whose beauty rivals great works of art and whose wisdom compares to the sacred teachings of the world's religions? Both Jung and Hillman insist that the symbolic imagery of dreaming can bring forth profound meanings and powerful healing energies—if waking consciousness can surrender its inflated self-image and enter into a true dialogue with the unconscious.

The sharp disagreement between these two approaches is unnecessary, Hunt says, because both approaches are right about different types of dreams. Foulkes, Hobson, and Freud are right that cognitively sophisticated narrative and grammatical processes are primary in the shaping of many dreams (such as personal-mnemonic dreams). But Jung and Hillman are also right that spontaneous, highly creative visual-spatial imagery often appears in dreams and takes the lead in forming the rarer "intensified" types of dreams. Hunt says that in most cases both cognitive modes, the narrative-grammatical and the visual-spatial, are working together, combining and interacting in many different ways to form the various types of dreaming experience: "We arrive then at a picture of two systems, both self-referential and creatively recombinatory expressions of the human symbolic capacity, interacting in different measures to produce both normative dreaming and its imagistically predominant variations" (168).

Hunt offers one of his own dreams (which occurred while he was in the process of separating from his wife) to illustrate how strange, unexpected visual-spatial elements do not necessarily disrupt the grammatical structure and thematic continuity of a dream but may actually enhance the dream's dramatic sense, fulfilling and completing its narrative intention.

I am traveling with my wife and children, looking for a parking place in order to visit the Tibetan National Museum. The only parking areas I can find are in highway rest areas and I realize that unless I hurry the museum will close. Accordingly, I now drive directly to the museum (a huge building with multiple wings and four or five floors). Leaving my car and family in front, I run inside. I enter a massive foyer and find to my intense disappointment that the museum has just closed. Looking about, I notice an open door to a small room off to one side. Entering, I find myself in the private apartment of an older, very thin women, who is apparently the museum caretaker. The room is primitive and archaic. The women is in one corner steadily stirring a very large pot of boiling water. As I approach more closely I see in the pot a carved wooden manikin about two feet tall. As the woman stirs, ignoring me, the room is filled with an eerie, high-pitched wailing sound. I realize with growing horror that the sound emanates from the wooden manikin, which is becoming progressively more lifelike as she stirs—its scream of pain becomes more and more shrill and frenzied and then begins to turn into an uncanny and strangely beautiful song. I realize that the price of the vivification of the manikin is the terrible agony that produces this song, and I awaken in a cold sweat. (166, spelling mistakes in the original)

Hunt points to the sharp discontinuity in this dream between the initial scene of driving around with his family in search of a parking place and the final scene of hearing the little manikin's agonized scream turned into a beautiful song. Foulkes would likely see such a radical shift in both character and setting as another instance of the random, meaningless disruptions so common in dreams. But Hunt argues that the two scenes, in fact, combine to enhance the overall psychological power of the dream. The first scene establishes a contrast between his family responsibilities and his personal interests in Tibetan culture, a contrast that seems to have symbolic relations to his impending marital separation. The second scene develops that contrast further, expanding it into a symbolic polarity of dying and coming alive, "with the further implication that such a coming alive will be mediated by the feminine and, of course, by immense pain" (167). In this case, then, the apparent discontinuity and bizarreness actually helped "to weld this dream together as a single dramatic whole. . . . [It] constitutes a powerful metaphor for a major dilemma and an acute anticipation of its resolution" (167).

Hunt's research indicates that there are a number of relatively distinct types of dreaming. Each of these different dream types is formed by a different combination of cognitive processes, and each dream type has its own line of potential development. Hunt admits that the "multiplicity of dreams" makes scientific research quite difficult, because investigators must be sensitive to the overlap and interplay of all the various dream types. (For an example of the benefits of this kind of approach, see Knudson and Minier 1999 and Knudson 2001.) Furthermore, investigators must take into account the many factors (physiological, psychological, and cultural) that promote the experience of some dream types and inhibit the experience of other types. In modern Western culture, for example, personal-mnemonic dreams are considered normal, while reports of medical-somatic and prophetic dreams are often greeted with disbelief and ridicule. Hunt believes these cultural attitudes have a subtle but powerful impact on the development of the cognitive processes involved in dreaming.

For this reason, Hunt is skeptical about absolutist claims regarding the function of dreaming: "There may not be a fundamental function of dreaming, any more than we can find a function for human existence generally. . . . It may be because dreaming has no fixed function that it is open to so many different uses" (76).

Ernest Hartmann on Nightmares and the Boundaries of the Mind

Ernest Hartmann was a psychiatrist who taught at Tufts University Medical School and directed the Sleep Research Laboratory at Lemuel

Shattuck Hospital in Boston. Among his many books are *The Biology of Dreaming* (1967), *Sleep and Dreaming* (1970), and *The Functions of Sleep* (1973). In 1984 he published *The Nightmare: The Psychology and Biology of Terrifying Dreams*, which combines clinical and experimental studies to examine the questions of who has nightmares and why. In formulating his answers to these questions, Hartmann develops the key notion of "boundaries of the mind." He argues that frequent nightmare sufferers have "thin" psychological boundaries, which makes them more vulnerable to anxiety-filled dreams. (He gives a more detailed account of this notion in his 1991 book, *Boundaries of the Mind*, and in his 1999 work, *Dreams and Nightmares*.)

Hartmann's research shows that there are two very different frightening dream phenomena: the *nightmare* and the *night terror*. He offers as an example of a night terror the following report from a subject in a sleep laboratory experiment:

> Fifty minutes after sleep onset during stage 4 NREM sleep, a body movement occurs, HS [the subject] rolls over screaming repeatedly, "Help, help." He mutters about swallowing something and choking. His pulse rate has increased from 60 to 90 per minute during the 15 seconds it takes him to awaken. He quickly falls asleep again, and later has no recall for the event. (1984, 11)

As an example of a nightmare, Hartmann recounts this experience of a woman awakened in his sleep lab at 7:50 a.m., after a 19-minute-long REM period:

> I was at my parents' house and they had gone out to some party . . . or something like that and I was home alone. Suddenly, this guy from next door came over and he just kind of walked through the house. And I asked him what he needed and he told me he was having trouble moving his house. And it turned out that he was having some kind of legal trouble so that he had to move his house a certain number of feet. And in the dream I went out into the yard and he had moved his whole house and it crashed into my parents' house. . . . I got really scared and I started to run. And this other guy ran after me and caught me . . . and I kept struggling. (14)

Hartmann explains that night terrors occur during stages 3 or 4 NREM sleep, usually within the first two hours following sleep onset. They involve sudden arousal, screaming, sweating, and troubles with breathing. There is little or no imagery associated with the experience, and the person often does not recall it when fully awakened. Night terrors are not, strictly speaking, dreams at all. Hartmann says they are better understood as "disorders of arousal" (20). Nightmares, however, are very different experiences from night terrors. Hartmann says nightmares tend to be long, frightening dreams occurring during REM sleep, most often during the later parts of the night, that awaken the person with their vivid, clearly remembered imagery.

A third category of frightening dream, different from both nightmares and night terrors, is the *post-traumatic nightmare*. These frightening dreams are provoked by a terrible waking-life experience (e.g., wartime combat, car crash, sexual assault, natural disaster, terrorist attack). The waking-life experience is then replayed in frighteningly direct and graphic detail in the person's dreams, over and over again. In some cases, the nightmares continue to plague the person decades after the original traumatic experience. However, Hartmann says that with most post-traumatic nightmares the repetitions fade rapidly, especially if the person is able to talk about the experience and make some progress in integrating it into the rest of his or her life:

> A typical story here is after a traumatic event, the event may be dreamt almost literally a few times and then gradually other elements are included as the event becomes woven into the rest of one's dream life—"I was with some friends at this place we used to have near New York. Some kind of party; and then those guys came in who looked like the guys who attacked me last month, except in the dream they were wearing these funny old-fashioned suits. I was kind of scared, but I kept talking to my girlfriend, and ignored them." (192)

Post-traumatic nightmares may occur during any stage of sleep, indicating that they are "a third psychophysiological entity, not identical to either ordinary nightmares or night terrors" (188). (For more on the various types of nightmares, see Adler 2011, Hurd 2010, Hufford 1982, Revonsuo 2003, Nielsen and Levin 2007.)

To explain why some people frequently suffer from long, terrifying dreams, Hartmann uses the notion of "boundaries of the mind." The natural development of mental structures that begins in childhood involves learning to distinguish between self and other, inside and outside, fantasy and reality, and other basic features of life. Each of these distinctions implies psychological realms with boundaries around them. Using data from both clinical and experimental research, Hartmann argues that frequent nightmare sufferers have "thin or permeable boundaries":

> They may form less firm ego boundaries, less solid boundaries around their feeling of self, and less firm interpersonal boundaries among others. These people are painfully sensitive to, and in danger from, their own wishes and impulses as well as demands or threats from the world outside. Indeed, the childhood histories obtained from the nightmare sufferers are those of persons who were always unusually sensitive, unusually open and vulnerable, and thus to some extent felt different from others. They often have had a painful and sometimes lonely childhood followed by a stormy and difficult adolescence. As they became adults, some of them—and this is more true of women—were able to maintain the openness inherent in a thin-boundary condition and were able to apply it in their work as artists, teachers, or therapists, but it was a difficult state to maintain and they were sometimes vulnerable to psychosis and also to physical injury. (158)

In contrast to people with "thick boundaries," who have stronger defenses against threats from the outer world and from unconscious fears and impulses, people with thin boundaries are more easily overwhelmed by both externally and internally generated threats—resulting in a greater vulnerability to frequent nightmares.

Occasional nightmares are normal for all people, those with thin as well as thick boundaries. Young children have the most nightmares of any age group. (And young children are also especially prone to experience night terrors.) Hartmann estimates that the average incidence of nightmares among adults is one to two per year. Certain factors tend to increase nightmare frequency: various medications (especially L-dopa, used in the treatment of Parkinson's disease), physical or mental illnesses, and in general, any kind of major life stress or trauma. Hartmann says that, for all people, "nightmares appear to be especially frequent in situations that involve helplessness or that remind a person of childhood feelings of helplessness" (36).

Hartmann's research has pointed to some important connections between thin psychological boundaries and dreaming. People who have thin boundaries (as determined by their scores on a battery of psychological tests) remember far more dreams than do those who have thick boundaries. Furthermore, people with thin boundaries have dreams that are more vivid, detailed, and emotional than are the dreams of people with thick boundaries. Hartmann has argued that dreaming itself can be considered a thin-boundary state, characterized by openness, fluidity, and ambiguity. In his view, the basic nature of dreaming is that it makes psychological connections more broadly than does waking thought. These connections are not the products of a random process, but are guided by the dominant emotional concerns of the dreamer.

Factors Influencing Dream Recall

The question of why people remember some of their dreams and not others has puzzled almost every modern dream psychologist. Freud, for example, said dreams are never intended to be remembered because of the deceptive workings of the censor, so it should be no surprise that people rarely recall their dreams. Jung replied that low dream recall is due not to an internal censor, but rather to the inability of rational waking consciousness to understand the special symbolic images and themes typically expressed in dreams.

As with so much in the modern psychology of dreaming, the findings of sleep laboratory research cast an entirely new light on this question. According to psychologist Kathryn Belicki, whose research frames the following discussion, when subjects sleeping in the laboratory are awakened during a REM period, they recall a dream approximately 80 percent of the time, or four to five dreams per night (1987, 187). However, these same people recall on average only two to three dreams per week when sleeping normally at home. These findings have greatly added to the mystery surrounding the question of dream recall. It now seems that everyone is dreaming many times every night but forgetting the vast majority of these dream experiences upon awakening.

Cognitive psychologists who study the nature of memory have suggested that one major impediment to dream recall is the general difficulty of retrieving from memory storage any experience that occurs during sleep. But, as Belicki notes, this still leaves open the question of why people occasionally do remember their dreams. It also leaves open the question of why certain people tend to remember many of their dreams, while other people virtually never remember their dreams.

Research indicates that at least four different factors influence the daily variations in each individual's dream recall (see Schredl 2007). First is the condition under which people are awakened from sleep. If people are immediately distracted when they wake up (by an alarm clock, other people, pressing concerns about school or work), then they are much less likely to recall their dreams than if they wake up in a slow, quiet, and unhurried fashion. Second is motivation. People recall many more dreams when they have some special interest in the subject, perhaps because they are taking a psychology class or reading a book on dreams or seeing a psychotherapist. Third is the characteristics of the particular dream. Dreams that occur toward the end of the night seem to be more easily recalled the next morning than dreams occurring earlier in the sleep cycle. And long, intense dreams are much better remembered than short, less intense dreams. The fourth factor is life stress. In many cases, dream recall increases during times of stress and crisis. This effect of stress on dream recall seems especially strong among women. The association of stress with other demographic factors (such as low socio-economic status) may adversely impact dream recall frequencies for many people (see Arber et al. 2009; 2012).

Turning to the question of why some people recall a high proportion of their dreams while other people recall a much lower proportion, one widespread theory is that people who have a generally defensive personality tend to remember fewer of their dreams. Another theory holds that people who possess highly developed powers of imagination—whose cognitive style involves a greater openness and ability to use imagery and creative processes while awake—tend to remember more of their dreams. But Belicki says both of these theories should be regarded with caution:

> A major problem that exists with all the research on personality and ability factors is that the observed relationships tend to be disappointingly small. One possible reason for this state of affairs is that it has been widely assumed that differences among people in dream recall are stable differences, consistent over time. However, in my early research when I regularly asked subjects to estimate their typical weekly dream recall, many individuals would insist they did not have a typical amount of recall, that their recall fluctuated dramatically from one time period to the next. (197–198)

Setting aside competing theories, there are some solid empirical findings in this area of research that can be summarized as follows. Almost all humans remember at least some of their dreams. Very few people, perhaps less than 1 percent of the population, have never recalled any dreams (Pagel 2010). Average dream recall rates are about one or two per week for most people. Children and young people tend to remember dreams more often than do older people, and females tend to have higher recall than males. A positive attitude toward dreaming can enhance recall, and a negative attitude can diminish or suppress recall (Schredl 2007; Beaulieu-Prevost and Zadra 2005, 2007). The role of personal attitudes about dreams as a factor in dream recall can help account for the general effectiveness of cross-cultural rituals of dream incubation, which seek to elicit a revelatory dream about an important topic of personal concern (Patton 2004).

Perhaps the most important point to take from this review is that any psychological theory attempting to explain the function of dreaming must account for the wide variation in dream recall. Most people regularly forget almost all of their dream experiences, but most people also regularly remember at least a few of those dreams. Some people remember numerous dreams every night, while other people rarely remember any dreams. Some dreams are wispy and evaporate from memory soon after waking, while others are overwhelmingly powerful and impossible to forget.

Cognitive Psychology's Answers to the Three Basic Questions

Formation

Cognitive psychologists generally agree that what we experience as dreams are constructed and shaped by the same basic mental operations that are at work in our conscious waking thought. For Piaget, dreaming is best understood in terms of the fundamental psychological tendencies toward accommodation and assimilation. Hall emphasizes the continuity between dream content and waking-life thoughts, concerns, and conceptions. Foulkes focuses on the identities in dreaming and waking thought processes, especially language formation. Hunt discusses the role in dreams of both narrative-grammatical and visual-spatial cognitive processes. Hartmann speaks of boundaries of the mind that structure waking and dreaming experiences. Cognitive psychologists also agree that as these basic mental operations develop from childhood into adulthood, so does dreaming: the dreams of adults are more complex and sophisticated than the dreams of children.

Functions

Most cognitive psychologists agree that dreaming plays some important role in the mind's ongoing effort to process both external and internal information, though much remains unknown about how exactly this works. In general, dreaming serves to promote the general adaptation of people to their waking environment, helping them to organize their perceptions, exercise their cognitive powers, and integrate new experiences with past memories. Some cognitive psychologists (e.g., Hunt) argue that dreaming may also provide people with stunningly original and creatively meaningful metaphors that speak directly to their major waking-life concerns.

Interpretation

Cognitive psychologists like Foulkes are skeptical regarding attempts to interpret what particular dreams might mean. Others, however, are more willing to use their research to guide efforts at dream interpretation. Hall stresses the importance of interpreting whole series of dreams; knowing the basic features of the series as a whole can be of great help in determining what any single dream in the series might mean. For Hunt, the existence of multiple types of dreams requires interpreters to be careful not to misapply models appropriate for understanding one type of dream in trying to understand a different type of dream. Most cognitive psychologists offer their research not as an interpretive system in itself, but as a source of empirical data about dreams and dreaming from which anyone involved in the practice of dream interpretation can benefit.

Popular Psychology: Bringing Dreams to the People

The IASD supports an approach to dreamwork and dream sharing that respects the dreamer's dignity and integrity, and which recognizes the dreamer as the decision-maker regarding the significance of the dream. Systems of dreamwork that assign authority or knowledge of the dream's meanings to someone other than the dreamer can be misleading, incorrect, and harmful. Ethical dreamwork helps the dreamer work with his/her own dream images, feelings, and associations, and guides the dreamer to more fully experience, appreciate, and understand the dream. Every dream may have multiple meanings, and different techniques may be reasonably employed to touch these multiple layers of significance.

—From the Dreamwork Ethics Statement of the International Association for the Study of Dreams, 1997

Historical surveys of modern dream psychology often neglect to mention the contributions of people whose work focuses on teaching psychological theories and practices of dreaming to the general public. This is unfortunate, because these "pop psychologists" have genuinely advanced our knowledge of dreams by exploring the dream lives of ordinary people outside the limited and often artificial contexts of the psychotherapy office and the sleep laboratory. The teachers, writers, and caregivers who work in this broad realm are carrying on the tradition of Artemidorus, the Greek dream interpreter who, almost 2,000 years ago, made a careful and respectful study of the dream lives of the common folk.

A number of currents came together in North America and Western Europe in the 1960s and early 1970s to form a broad-based popular psychological approach to dreaming. By this time, the teachings of Freud and Jung had been disseminated widely enough that their basic ideas about dreams, symbols, and the unconscious were familiar to a significant percentage of the population. The discoveries of the sleep lab had been publicized with great enthusiasm by newspapers and magazines, and these media reports put special emphasis on the finding that *all* humans have regular amounts of REM sleep, indicating that all humans dream every night. The counter-culture movement of the 1960s had stimulated many people's interest in altered states of consciousness, which could be experienced through dreams as well as drugs, music, and meditation. And reports from anthropologists about the dream practices of non-Western cultures (such as Native Americans, Australian aborigines, and African tribespeople) began reaching popular audiences, describing how people in these cultures cherish their dreams as powerful wellsprings of spiritual wisdom, artistic creativity, and guidance in both personal and communal life.

A group of psychologists took these different sources of information about dreams and, with the help of newly developed techniques of mass-market communication, addressed the practical interests and concerns of people throughout the population. This chapter describes their major works and their contributions to modern dream psychology.

Self-Help Books on Dreams: Ann Faraday, Patricia Garfield, Gayle Delaney

A wave of popular interest in dreams was generated in the late 20th century in large part by the work of three psychologists: Ann Faraday, Patricia Garfield, and Gayle Delaney. All three wrote highly successful mass-market books on dreams that aimed at giving general readers simple, practical, "how-to" suggestions for understanding their dreams.

Faraday's *Dream Power* (1972) begins with one of her own childhood dreams:

> When I was a small child, I used to have recurring dreams of being pursued by "Creamers"—men wearing long white coats and tall white hats—whose leader was named Beasley. I remember asking my mother what Creamers were, and she replied, "I think they're chocolates, darling." But I knew they weren't—they were men dressed in white who chased me throughout the night. (13)

Faraday's interest in dreams remained strong, and she eventually pursued graduate research in a sleep laboratory on frequencies of dream recall.

But her research disappointed her—"I learned much about rats, reaction time, and statistics, but nothing about myself" (1972, 14). Then, after a "totally frustrating experience of Freudian analysis which did violence both to me and to my dreams by trying to fit us into a rigid, limited, and dogmatic theory" (1974, xiii) and after an experience of Jungian analysis that was only slightly less negative, Faraday decided to develop her own approach to dreaming and dream interpretation. *Dream Power* was the result.

The book outlines Faraday's approach to "the use of dreams at home," which she calls "The Three Faces of Dreaming." According to this approach, dreams should always be looked at in three different ways:

> Looking outward, they [dreams] often bring to our attention things we have failed to notice in waking life. Second, we may use them as mirrors that reflect our attitudes and prejudices, and finally, by looking inward and treating the dream as an existential message about the state of our inner world, we can often discover the hidden source of our problems and regain long-buried aspects of the personality. (1972, 16)

In the final section of *Dream Power*, Faraday looks forward to what the use of dreams for greater self-knowledge could mean for families, churches, schools, business, politics, and society as a whole—"I believe this last part of the 20th century is likely to be marked by all kinds of experiments in new ways of promoting self-understanding and emotional growth, and I am sure that the use of dreams has an enormous part to play in this" (1972, 269). She also discusses the potential of dreams to provide creative inspiration, reveal profound spiritual truths, and open the door to ecstatic, transcendental experiences similar to other altered states of consciousness.

The Dream Game (1974) offers a more detailed set of practical instructions to help people understand their dreams better. Faraday describes how to keep a dream diary, how to interpret common dream themes, and how to ask for help from dreams through the practice of dream incubation (going to sleep with a specific question in mind and then interpreting that night's dream as a response to that question). Faraday chose the title *The Dream Game* for this book to emphasize her eclectic, playful approach to the various ways of interpreting dreams. For example, she shows her readers how to play the "Freudian game" of looking for sexual symbols and the "Jungian game" of looking for archetypal symbols. Faraday's own preference is for the "Gestalt game" of looking for topdog-underdog symbols and conflicts, and she devotes much of the book to recounting lively, insight-rich Gestalt dialogues between dreamers and different characters from their dreams. But as helpful as all these various dream games may be, Faraday insists, "None of these, nor any other way of working with dreams, is universally true; and we do violence to our dreams if we try to force them into restricting theories" (1974, xvii).

Patricia Garfield's *Creative Dreaming* (1974) is aimed at helping people plan and control their dreams so they can unify their personalities, deal better with waking-life fears and problems, and become more creative in all they do. Garfield first started keeping a dream diary when she was 14, and she says that throughout her graduate studies in clinical psychology, her marriage, her parenting, her divorce, and her second marriage, "I found that my dreams were a source of self-reflection and understanding. They helped support me through difficult times" (1988, xi). She wrote *Creative Dreaming* to share her experiences and insights with others:

> The prevailing idea [at this time] was that dreams are experiences occurring during sleep that only afterwards may be analyzed and worked with by professionals. Dreams were out of the province of the average dreamer; it was said that they could not be influenced by the dreamer and that dream style changed little over a lifetime. I knew this was not true. Working with my own dreams since my teenage years had taught me much about myself. Each dreamer, I believed, could benefit from understanding his or her own dreams. (1988, xii)

Creative Dreaming differs from Faraday's two books in that it draws more heavily on historical and cross-cultural sources. Garfield provides lengthy narrative accounts of the dream practices of ancient Greeks, Native Americans, Malaysian tribespeople, and Tibetan Buddhists. She says that in many of these cultures people developed the ability to become conscious within their dreams, and thus to control what happens in their dream worlds. This wonderful ability allows people to fearlessly approach whatever threatens them in their dreams, transforming fear and weakness into power and strength. Garfield says that such exhilarating experiences of dream control and creativity "produce a mood of capability that carries over into waking life, providing a foundation for confident, capable action" (1974, 14).

Synthesizing the teachings of these different cultures, Garfield says that anyone can learn to become a creative dreamer. The crucial starting point is to take dreams seriously and to recognize that becoming conscious within a dream is indeed possible:

> In every system we have reviewed, the dreamer's attitude is of prime importance. Creative dreaming is rather like believing in the possibility of

love; if you have never experienced it, it is difficult to believe it can exist for you. Once love has become a reality for you, no cynic on earth can persuade you that it does not exist. So it is with creative dreaming. Once you have been fully conscious during a dream, you *know* it can be done. (1974, 199)

Garfield goes on to give detailed instructions on how to develop consciousness within the dream state. She says people should go to sleep in a quiet, peaceful condition and focus their pre-sleep attention on the specific goal of becoming aware within their dreams. It may take a great deal of time and practice, but she says that eventually the experience of creative dreaming can come to anyone.

Gayle Delaney's *Living Your Dreams* (1979) explains the nature of dreaming by means of a film metaphor (similar to Jung's theater metaphor): dreams are "movies of the mind" in which the individual dreamer is the producer, the screenwriter, the director, and the star of each dream (xi, 5–7). Delaney opens her book with a dream she experienced after several years in Jungian analysis:

It was a beautiful night. The stars glittered excitingly in a navy blue satin sky. Oh, those stars! They twinkled with the spirit of an Irish Setter wagging his tail with joy at the return of his master. Here I was in Hollywood. I felt welcome and happy and full of expectations that something good was about to happen. The next thing I knew, I was being led into the spectacular home of Otto Preminger [a producer and director of several Hollywood films in the 1940s and 1950s]. I had never seen it before. Now, as I sat in the main living room, I savored its beauty. The room was decorated in the best Art Deco style. There were circular mirrors, palm trees, and blue silks covering great furniture forms. Everything was designed with symmetry and yet surprise. I was surrounded by luxurious and brilliant design reminiscent of some Fred Astaire and Ginger Rogers movie set. I awaited the entrance of the great movie producer. What would he say to me? Why was I invited to come here? Would he say, 'I want to make you a star'? Would I be able at last to ice skate and dance my heart out in the movies? I kept waiting for Mr. Preminger to walk into the room. I waited, and waited . . . and waited. Slowly, slowly, I began to realize that this marvelous house belonged to me! Somehow Otto Preminger's house was mine! (1979, 4)

Delaney says this dream helped her stop looking at her dreams as something she received from outside, and start experiencing them as her own creations. To her, Otto Preminger was the greatest movie producer of all time, so his house becoming *her* house meant that she was the "Otto Preminger" of her own dream productions.

With this as her starting point, Delaney devotes her book to describing techniques to help people be more effective in directing their dream productions and more successful in understanding the messages conveyed by their private cinematic creations. After presenting basic techniques on keeping a dream diary and practicing dream incubation (she calls her method "phrase focusing or secular dream incubation" [20]), Delaney outlines her "dream interview" approach to interpreting dreams.

She says the best way to begin grasping the meaning of a dream is to ask the dreamer simply to describe and define the dream's imagery. Delaney says, "You may find the producer more willing to answer your questions if you first ask him to pretend that you come from another planet" (52). In this way, the dreamer is encouraged to become aware of the special ideas, beliefs, and associations he or she has in relation to a particular dream image. For example, if a person dreams of a dog, the interviewer would say, "Pretend I'm from another planet and don't know what a dog is. Can you describe a 'dog' to me?" The dreamer might say a dog has four legs, has a good sense of smell, makes a barking sound, and is very faithful—and then the dreamer might suddenly realize the dog in the dream connects to a waking-life problem having to do with faithfulness.

The goal of the dream interview method is to help the dreamer discover the connections or bridges between the dream and waking life. Delaney emphasizes that "it is appallingly easy to misinterpret another's dreams," and she warns interviewers to be careful about forcing their interpretations onto the dreamer (53). She encourages people to practice her methods, to see how easy it can be to interpret dreams: "Most dreams will yield their messages to a skilled interviewer with surprisingly little effort" (56).

These self-help books by Faraday, Garfield, and Delaney have sold hundreds of thousands of copies worldwide, aided in large part by the authors' skills in communicating their ideas through television, radio, magazines, and other mass-media outlets. The commercial success of their books reflects a strong interest among the general public for new ideas and practices in the psychology of dreaming. Their books have also given other dream researchers a great deal of food for thought. Faraday, Garfield, and Delaney have shown that people who are not in formal psychotherapy can learn and fruitfully apply simple principles of dream interpretation. They have shown that dreams can give people valuable insights to help deal with common waking-life problems (such as troubles with family, work, health, etc.). And, they have shown that becoming more aware of dreams can enhance people's self-esteem, creativity, and spiritual vitality.

Dream-Sharing Groups: Montague Ullman and Jeremy Taylor

Although Faraday, Garfield, and Delaney all discuss the sharing of dreams in group settings, the practice has been most fully developed by Montague Ullman and Jeremy Taylor.

Ullman was a psychoanalytically trained psychiatrist who founded the Dream Laboratory at the Maimonides Medical Center in New York. In the 1960s, his work in community psychiatry led him to consider various ways in which mental health services could be brought to communities where such services were unavailable. Then in the 1970s, Ullman went to Sweden to help develop a psychoanalytic training program and pursue further work in community mental health. In both countries, Ullman focused his efforts on teaching people his methods of group "dream appreciation" (Ullman and Zimmerman 1979, 12). In Sweden, he actually received government sponsorship and funding to support community dream-sharing groups. Ullman said his basic approach to working with dreams in group settings derives from two basic facts about dreams:

> First, it is useful to have support as we struggle to bring an honest perspective to our dreams. Second, others who are not personally involved in the dream can often "read" our metaphors better than we can, simply because they do not have to deal with the consequences of their reading. (Ullman and Zimmerman 1979, 13)

In his 1979 book, *Working with Dreams*, co-authored with Nan Zimmerman, Ullman lays out a five-stage process for working with dreams in groups. In the first stage, the dreamer shares the dream with the group. In the second, the group reflects on the feelings, images, and metaphors they perceive and the empathetic connections they find within the dream. During this stage, the dreamer remains silent and simply listens while the group responds to the dream. Ullman emphasizes that all the responses are useful, even the "'wrong ones,' because a 'wrong' response helps the dreamer define what the image is not and thereby may help the dreamer get closer to defining what it is" (217). After the group has considered every detail of the dream, the dreamer is invited in the third stage to respond to the group's responses. A dialogue between the group and the dreamer ensues in the fourth stage, and the fifth and final stage has the dreamer reflecting on final comments about all the meanings that have come up during the group process. Ullman says,

> If the group members have been successful they have functioned as midwives; they have brought the dream out to public view and helped

establish the dreamer's connection to it. When this happens their job is finished and the job of the one who gave birth to the dream begins in earnest. (220)

Jeremy Taylor, a Unitarian Universalist minister, did his first formal group dream sharing while he was leading a consciousness-raising seminar on racism (as part of his alternative civilian service as a conscientious objector to the Vietnam War). As Taylor describes it in *Dream Work* (1983), when he suggested that the seminar members share and discuss their dreams in which black people appeared,

> The energy for growth and transformation of personality and unconscious attitudes and fears that were released by this work was truly astonishing, even to me. The dream work was effective in bringing deep-seated unconscious ambivalences to light, and the work was further effective in transforming them, because each of us was forced to "own" both the negative and positive images of black people in our dreams as representations of aspects of our own personalities. (16)

Taylor says the tremendous value of group dream sharing derives from the fact that, by hearing the comments and reflections of a variety of different people, the dreamer "is exposed to a fuller range of the dream's possible meanings" (76). Because every dream has more than one meaning, a dream-sharing group provides excellent opportunities for exploring those multiple meanings, more than can usually be discovered by working on dreams alone or with only one other person.

While dream-sharing groups can take many different forms, Taylor recommends the following structures and principles to guide any group:

- The group (ideally 6 to 12 people) gathers in a quiet, comfortable place.
- One of the people serves as leader or facilitator for the group, monitoring the flow of discussion and watching the time.
- After an initial "touch-in" to discuss how everyone is doing, each person in the group describes a dream.
- The group chooses one person's dream to discuss in detail and proceeds to offer comments, ask questions, and suggest meanings regarding the dream.
- This discussion can take from 15 minutes to 2 hours; usually, an effort is made to discuss more than one dream at a given meeting.
- Over the course of a few meetings, everyone in the group participates. Everyone gets to share his or her own dreams, everyone gets to comment on other people's dreams, and everyone gets to have a dream discussed by the group.

Taylor says the "only reliable touchstone of dream work" is the "aha!" or "tingle" feeling people get when they recognize a truth or meaning in their dreams. He argues that dream interpretation requires people to pay attention "with as much of [their] whole being as possible," so that these flashes of intuitive discovery can be perceived and understood (83). However, Taylor cautions that the "aha!" test should be balanced with critical self-awareness:

> One of the most important things to understand about group dream work is that the flashes and tingles and "ahas" you feel are always signals of truth, but that it is always a truth about *oneself*, and not necessarily a truth about the other person's dream. Thus, it is always true that what is said about someone else's dream reflects the personality and symbol structure of the person making the comment as much as or more than it reflects anything in the dream itself. For this reason it is often useful to preface any remark with the idea, "if it were *my* dream." (83)

Taylor says this "if it were *my* dream" preface helps to remind everyone in the group that the dream belongs to the dreamer, that only the dreamer knows for sure what the dream means, and that the other group members are engaged in a process of projecting their own ideas, feelings, and intuitions onto the dreamer's experience.

Suppose, for example, that a person shares a dream of driving a car too fast and realizing with fear that the brakes don't work. If a group member says, "*Your* dream means *your* life is speeding out of control," the comment may come across as authoritative, confrontational, and rude. But if the group member says, "If it were *my* dream, it would mean that *my* life is speeding out of control," the comment gives the dreamer more space to reflect on the interpretation. It also encourages the group member to reflect on his or her *own* feelings as they have been stimulated by the other person's dream. The "if it were *my* dream" preface clearly marks the comment as the group member's personal projection—a projection that may turn out to be extremely helpful to the dreamer. Taylor notes, "Even though we can do nothing but project ourselves into the understanding of other people's dreams, these projections often prove to be the source of insight for the dreamer" (83–84).

Taylor says the value of group dream sharing goes beyond giving people better insights into their dreams. As his racism seminar demonstrated, sharing dreams with other people has political and social value in helping overcome the barriers of race, age, sex, and class. By revealing one's own deepest hopes and fears, by giving insights into the deepest hopes and fears of other people, and by demonstrating how projections both hinder and enhance creative human relations, dream-sharing groups promote both personal and communal transformation: "The deep sense of community which group dream work creates continues to sustain and nurture the individual's creativity and courage, without which collective change is impossible" (17).

Lucid Dreaming: Stephen Laberge

Lucid dreaming is the ability to become aware within a dream that one is dreaming. In Western culture, this ability was recognized at least as early as the time of Aristotle (see chapter 1), was noted in passing by Freud (see chapter 2), and was discussed at some length in the books of all the aforementioned popular psychologists. But only in the last few years have scientific researchers begun making a truly detailed and systematic study of lucid dreams. The pioneer in this field is Stephen LaBerge, whose book *Lucid Dreaming* (1985) explains his psychophysiological research on lucid dreams to a mass-market audience. Keith Hearne was also doing similar kinds of laboratory research on lucid dreaming in England during the same period, but LaBerge wrote the first major publications on lucid dreaming as measured by the EEG. Later works covering the field of lucid dreaming research include Gackenbach and LaBerge's edited work, *Conscious Mind, Sleeping Brain* (1988); Purcell et al.'s work on "Waking, Dreaming, and Self-Regulation" (1993); Kahan and LaBerge's studies of metacognitive similarities and differences between waking and dreaming (2013); and Hurd and Bulkeley's edited book, *Lucid Dreaming* (2014).

LaBerge had experienced lucid dreams from the age of five, and as he grew up, he became increasingly fascinated by the phenomenon. In 1977 he first read the book *Lucid Dreams* (1968) by British parapsychologist Celia Green. Green's work further stimulated LaBerge's interest, and he began keeping a journal that, after seven years, contained almost 900 lucid dream reports. The more he studied his own lucid dream experiences, the more he wanted to try to "communicate from the lucid dream to the outside world, *while* the dream was happening" (68). He soon thereafter entered a doctoral program in psychophysiology at Stanford University with the express intent of using sleep lab technology to achieve his goal of scientifically proving that lucid dreams really occur.

As LaBerge pursued his research, he found that most sleep and dream researchers did not accept that lucid dreams were really dreams, despite the historical testimony of people like Aristotle and contemporary reports from Celia Green, Ann Faraday, Patricia Garfield, and others. In large part, this resistance was due to an essentially philosophical belief that a person simply could not be asleep *and* conscious at the same time: to be asleep is, by definition, not to be conscious. For many mainstream psychologists, the very concept of "lucid dreaming" seemed a contradiction in terms.

To refute this skeptical argument, LaBerge devised an ingenious experiment. The standard tool of measurement in a sleep laboratory is the EEG machine, which measures eye movements during the various stages of sleep. LaBerge says,

> I knew that lucid dreamers could freely look in any direction they wished while in a lucid dream, because I had done this myself. It occurred to me that by moving my (dream) eyes in a recognizable pattern, I might be able to send a signal to the outside world when I was having a lucid dream. (68)

After a number of failed attempts, LaBerge finally succeeded in becoming lucid while dreaming in Stanford's sleep laboratory. Within his dream, he opened his eyes, held his finger in front of him, and moved it in a vertical line, following it carefully with his eyes. When he awoke, he and his colleagues checked the data from the EEG monitor that had been attached to LaBerge while he slept: "We observed two large eye movements on the polygraph record just before I awakened from a thirteen-minute REM period. Here, finally, was objective evidence that at least one lucid dream had taken place during what was clearly REM sleep!" (70). LaBerge and others soon replicated this experiment, demonstrating that within REM sleep a person can become conscious and make prearranged eye signals through an EEG monitor to outside observers.

The Senoi Controversy

A key source in the books of Faraday, Garfield, Taylor, and, to a lesser extent, Delaney, is an article by Kilton Stewart titled "Dream Theory in Malaya." The article was originally published in 1953, but it reached a vastly wider audience when it was reprinted in Charles Tart's bestselling anthology, *Altered States of Consciousness* (1969). In this article, Stewart describes his encounter with the dream beliefs and practices of the Senoi, a small tribal culture in Malaysia that he first learned of in 1935 while traveling with a scientific expedition. Stewart reports that the Senoi people enjoyed a remarkably pleasant and conflict-free life, with no violence, crime, or warfare to speak of. He attributes this astonishing degree of social and psychological harmony among the Senoi to their practice of sophisticated dream education and interpretation techniques. According to Stewart,

> Dream interpretation is a feature of child education and is the common knowledge of all Senoi adults. The average Senoi layman practices the psychotherapy of dream interpretation on his family and his associates as a regular feature of education and daily social intercourse. Breakfast in the Senoi house is like a dream clinic, with the father and older brothers listening to and analyzing the dreams of all the children. At the end of the family clinic the male population gathers in the council, at which the dreams of the older children and all the men in the community are reported, discussed, and analyzed. (193)

The Senoi teach their children that within their dreams they should always "advance and attack in the teeth of danger," fighting against antagonistic dream characters and calling for help from dream allies when necessary (195). Children are also taught to force their dream antagonists to give them a gift (e.g., a story, song, or dance) that the children can then share with the whole community upon awakening. In these ways, Senoi children learn to value their inner creativity, develop a strong sense of self-confidence, and become an active contributor to the well-being of the group.

Stewart illustrates these teachings with the story of a Senoi boy who dreamed he was attacked by a friend. Upon awakening the boy's father told him to describe the dream to his friend, which he did. The friend's father then told his son that he may have inadvertently offended the dreamer without knowing it and that he should give a present to the dreamer and try to be especially nice to him. The boy who had the dream was also instructed to fight back in future dreams and to defeat any dream character that used his friend's image as a disguise.

Observing the idyllic life of these rain-forest dwellers and their passionate devotion to their dreams, Stewart concludes that many of the ills of modern civilization are due to its failure to develop the kinds of creative dream awareness that are central to the Senoi culture. But Stewart also concludes that the Senoi techniques are ultimately so simple that anyone can grasp them. He writes, "Fifteen years of experimentation with these Senoi principles have convinced me that all men, regardless of their cultural development, might profit by studying them" (193). Stewart devoted much of the rest of his life to translating what he had learned from the Senoi into terms that he felt ordinary Westerners could understand.

Stewart's account of Senoi dream theory had a huge impact on the emerging popular psychology approach to dreaming. The appealing image of a "primitive" people who lived in a virtual paradise because of their careful attention to dreams gave powerful inspiration to many people in Western society who were just beginning to explore their own dream experiences. Garfield, who visited the Senoi in 1972, captures this mood of excitement in her *Creative Dreaming*: "By applying Senoi concepts of dream control, we can produce beautiful creations and solve problems at the same time as integrating our personalities . . . Perhaps the Senoi peacefulness, cooperation, and creativity will become more of a reality, too!" (111).

However, some scholars questioned the quality of Stewart's research, and in 1985, G. William Domhoff published *The Mystique of Dreams*, a critical analysis of Stewart's claims in the light of other anthropological research on the Senoi. Domhoff argues that Stewart romanticizes the Senoi and attributes to them beliefs they never actually held and methods they never actually practiced. Like many cultures around the world, the Senoi pay attention to their dreams, but Domhoff asserts there is no evidence the Senoi held "morning dream clinics" or taught principles of dream control to their children, as Stewart claims. Domhoff says,

> There seems to be no way, then, to avoid a rather mundane conclusion after weighing a great deal of anthropological evidence from a variety of sources: Senoi people do not have an unusual theory or practice of dreams. . . . The Senoi do not practice the so-called Senoi dream theory. (34, 65)

Domhoff explains the appeal of "Senoi dream theory" first of all as a product of Stewart's own charismatic personality and story-telling abilities. He grants that Stewart "may have come to the ideas [about dream control, etc.] in part from discussions with dream adepts in Senoi settlements, but the ideas were in fact his" (64). Despite his failings as an anthropologist, Stewart earns Domhoff's respect as a man who was passionately committed to using his knowledge of ritual practices of primitive tribes to help people struggling to find meaning in modern society. "For all his foibles," Domhoff says, "there is a magic about Kilton Stewart that transcends Senoi dream theory" (64).

Domhoff also offers a broader explanation for all the excitement over the Senoi, an explanation that refers to the nature of American society in the 1960s and 1970s. Domhoff traces the widespread acceptance of Stewart's writings about the Senoi to three sources: 1) the human potential movement (centered at the Esalen Institute), which publicized Senoi

practices as a means to expanded consciousness and greater social harmony; 2) protests against the Vietnam War, which focused attention on
the acute differences between American culture and the traditions of
southeast Asia; and 3) the glowing endorsements of Senoi dreaming by
popular psychologists like Faraday and Garfield. Domhoff says that, ultimately, the Senoi became a kind of allegory for many people living in this
turbulent period of history:

> Paradoxical as it may sound, I think that Senoi dream theory had a deep
> appeal for Americans at this time because it was a new application of our
> deepest and most ingrained beliefs about human nature presented in the
> context of an allegorical story about community and authenticity. Very
> simply, the "Senoi way of dreaming" actually rests on the unquestioned
> American belief in the possibility of shaping and controlling both the envi-
> ronment and human nature. For Americans, but not for most people, and
> certainly not for the Senoi, human nature is malleable and perfectible. We
> are what we make of ourselves. We can do it if we try. Senoi dream theory
> is an extension of that basic precept to the world of dreams. The fact that it
> is unwittingly presented in a mystique of the primitive only makes it all
> the more attractive. It is independent evidence for our convictions. (75)

The debates about Stewart, the Senoi, and "Senoi dream theory" continue to the present. Jeremy Taylor, for instance, argues that the anthropological reports cited by Domhoff were gathered in the years following
World War II, after the Senoi culture had been ravaged by the violent
intervention of foreign armies. Thus, Taylor doubts that the Senoi gave
completely forthcoming and honest accounts about their real dream practices and beliefs to these later anthropologists. He asks,

> If a group of superiorly armed foreigners from a totally different culture
> descended on your community and stuck you and your family in a stock-
> ade for a couple of years and actively prevented you from living your life
> the way you had always chosen to, would you be likely to "tell all" to those
> foreigners about your most intimate psycho-spiritual life and practices
> afterwards? I know I wouldn't, and I am not willing to assume any less
> about "native informants." (Taylor 1995, 32)

In the introduction to the second edition of her book *Pathway to Ecstasy*
(1989), Garfield responds to Domhoff's criticism by saying that the truth
about the Senoi will probably never be known. For her, the important
thing is that "the principles attributed to the Senoi are effective" (xxv).
She, Taylor, and many other popular psychologists agree that whatever

the Senoi originally practiced, the principles of dream control described by Stewart can be easily learned and effectively used by ordinary people living in modern Western society.

New Technologies, Networks, and Media

The early years of the 21st century have brought many new opportunities for spreading information about the psychology of dreaming to a broad public audience. The primary driver of these opportunities has been the emergence of the worldwide web, which has radically transformed the way we communicate, teach, work, play, and interact. Virtually every researcher, sleep laboratory, and dream-related organization has a website providing access to a wealth of materials, enabling people from any place with an internet connection to learn about current findings in dream psychology. For example, the International Association for the Study of Dreams (IASD) sponsors online conferences, organizes collaborative research projects, and offers many ways for people to connect digitally with academics, clinicians, artists, etc. all over the world (www.asdreams.org). Many other groups in dream research and education link to each other through the IASD, creating an extensive network of therapists and practitioners from a wide variety of backgrounds.

An ongoing challenge in the digital age, not only for dream researchers but for everyone who relies on internet resources, is how best to preserve the materials now available so they *remain* available going forward into the future. Many valuable websites have already come and gone without any documentation of their holdings. A greater degree of coordination among the various digital enterprises involved in the psychology of dreaming is vital to help preserve more of the valuable information being gathered and curated on their websites.

For research purposes, some of the greatest benefits of digital technology arise in improved capacities for gathering, analyzing, and archiving large collections of data relating to sleep and dreams. From the very beginning of the field, psychologists interested in dreams have tried to base their theories on some kind of empirical foundation, using as many dreams as they could manage to gather in a reliable form. New technologies have made it possible to accelerate this process dramatically, allowing researchers to perform quantitative analyses in a fraction of the time it used to take for such investigations. This bodes well for the future of dream psychology, especially if researchers are careful to use high-quality data from trustworthy and transparent sources.

The SDDb (http://sleepanddreamdatabase.org) has been developed with these principles in mind. It is intended to provide an online resource that supports both scientific research and personal exploration into the world of dreaming, inspired by the idea that these two approaches are not opposed but can mutually inform and enlighten each other. If it is true that all humans have an innate propensity to dream every night, it seems likely we also have an innate capacity to make sense of our dreams, too. By offering these digital technologies of dream research to experts and novices alike, I am hoping the SDDb will set the stage for creative sparks of new discovery in discerning the deeper patterns of meaning and significance in human dream experience.

Popular Psychology's Answers to the Three Basic Questions

Formation

Popular psychologists believe that all humans have dreams: dreaming is a normal, natural part of every person's life. This belief is based on the traditional teachings of cultures from around the world, on the findings of the modern sleep laboratory, and on the experiences of working closely with countless members of the general public. Popular psychologists agree that dreams are formed out of material from people's ordinary, daily life activities. They also agree that consciousness can play a large role in influencing and controlling dream content (such as in the cases of lucid dreaming and dream incubation). However, popular psychologists do not all agree on where the ultimate source of dream formation lies. Some, like Delaney and LaBerge, believe that dreams are created by the dreamer's mind alone. Others, like Faraday, Garfield, and Taylor, believe that at least some dreams are shaped by transpersonal forces.

Function

For popular psychologists, dreams have the potential to serve a variety of positive functions in the lives of ordinary people. Although each of the popular psychologists discussed in this chapter emphasizes some dream functions more than others, they all claim that dreams work to give deep insights into a person's emotional world, help solve important problems in daily life, provide indications about physical health (even offering early warnings about impending illnesses), promote the overall integration of one's personality, stimulate creativity, and reveal profound spiritual truths. Most of these psychologists also discuss the possibility that a greater awareness of dreams can promote not just individual welfare but also the resolution of problems and conflicts that plague society as a whole.

Interpretation

Popular psychologists focus most of their attention on giving detailed, practical instructions on how to interpret dreams. These instructions usually include advice on keeping a dream diary, suggestions about what typical dream themes frequently mean, and various techniques for connecting or bridging dream images to waking-life concerns. Most of these psychologists also describe how to practice dream incubation, how to become lucid while dreaming, how to share and interpret dreams in a group setting, and how to express and honor dream images in waking life. The popular psychology approach to dream interpretation is guided by the twin spirits of *eclecticism* and *democracy*: eclecticism in its willingness to use multiple methods of interpretation and its refusal to accept any one method as the best for all dreams and all dreamers, and democracy in its belief that everyone has the ability to interpret and benefit from his or her own dreams, without the need for analysts, therapists, scientists, priests, or any other outside experts.

Modern Psychology's Answers to the Three Basic Questions about Dreaming

I am at our original family house, and I see some cats I do not recognize walking around in the backyard. It looks like a mother and two kittens. I go around to the front of the house, and I see a couple of our cats, Strauss and another one. They are looking at something on the ground—a dead bird or something like that? At another point, I am in a kitchen with white walls and counters. Suddenly, I see the water outside has risen to a level right below the black-framed windows. Alarmed, I quickly latch the windows to keep the water from getting inside. A little water has already gotten in. I feel like I should have seen this coming, been more prepared. My wife said to be careful. At some point, I find out that someone else has published or made a public presentation about L.'s story. I am very upset and disappointed I did not get to present her story first.

—Author, August 10, 2016

One good way of evaluating the many different psychological theories about dreams and dreaming is to apply each of them in turn to a dream of one's own. Such an exercise brings forth the distinctive features of each theory and allows for critical reflection on their relative strengths and weaknesses. As this book has shown, the modern psychology of dreaming has grown in large part out of people's careful, disciplined examination of their own dreams. Beginning with the pioneering self-analyses of

Freud and Jung, psychologists have regularly drawn on their own dreams as one important resource in pursuing their research. This does, it must be admitted, give dream psychology the appearance of being subjective and unscientific. But the unavoidable fact is that our most direct means of access to the images, sensations, and emotions found in dreams is through our own dreams. Although debate about proper research methodology continues, most dream psychologists agree that if self-analysis is combined with solid findings from other research methods, there is nothing dangerous or unscientific about examining one's own dreams. Indeed, the history of modern dream psychology has demonstrated that many of the most creative breakthroughs have come from researchers who have developed innovative approaches to their personal dreaming experiences.

Psychological Analyses of a Sample Dream

The dream described at the outset of this chapter came to me during the summer, after a good night's sleep in my bed at home. Several associations immediately came to mind in relation to the dream's images. The house in the dream is where I and my wife and children lived for almost 20 years, before moving to another state a few years ago. The layout of the house and outside gardens is basically the same in the dream as in waking life. We have several cats, and among them, Strauss is the most skillful and prolific hunter. The kitchen does not reflect the actual kitchen from this house or any other familiar place, but it does seem to be "my" kitchen in the dream, in that I am responsible for it. The rising water immediately strikes me as unusual. I am surprised at its sudden rise, and even more surprised that such a huge volume of water does not come crashing into the house, rather than just trickling in. The situation does not fit with my sense of intuitive physics, and I'm aware of this in the dream and somewhat frightened by it.

The previous day, I had been mostly working outside, clearing brush and pruning trees at a forest property with a big creek where my wife and I are planning to eventually retire. I had recently met with a Fish and Wildlife Department official to discuss restoration work we are doing to promote healthier conditions for the salmon swimming through the creek. At some point, the official and I talked about a nearby sighting of a mountain lion a few months earlier. She and I also talked about putting up new signs to deter trespassers from using the access road across our property.

A few days before the dream, my wife and I watched the opening ceremony of the Summer Olympics held in Brazil. During the ceremony, mention was made of the dangers of global climate change, with some ominous statistics about rising ocean levels and forced population displacements. I had seen other statistics like these recently but my wife had not, and I was disturbed by her alarm at this troubling portrait of the environmental future; if she is worried, I should be *really* worried.

Earlier that day I had also done some writing for a manuscript involving a historical case study of a young woman (L.) with unusual dreams. After a year of intensive writing, I was getting close to the finish, although I still had lots to do in the few weeks left before the publisher's deadline. Happiness at nearing the end of the project was mixed with anxiety about getting my version of L.'s story out into the world before anyone else did. I had put a great deal of effort into my analysis and exploration of her case, and I worried the impact of this work would be diminished if someone else published a similar study before mine.

Freud

A Freudian approach to the dream would begin with these memories and associations and would use them as clues to finding the repressed unconscious wishes motivating the dream. Although an exhaustive analysis of these associations is impractical here (Freud's line-by-line examination of his "Dream of Irma's Injection" goes on for 14 pages), the following dream elements seem most striking. The initial setting of the dream, with the original family home and the mother cat with two kittens, harkens back to an earlier phase of life, when young children were at the center of my daily activities. The cats are unfamiliar, suggesting this is a fantasy setting, separate from current waking life. This pleasant fantasy of the past is disrupted by the actuality of a familiar cat (Strauss) and the harsh fact of death. The dream then shifts to the white kitchen, another protected fantasy setting with symbolic ties to home, childhood, and family nourishment.

At this point Freud would likely identify the kitchen with a womb, and he would suggest the dream is trying to fulfill an unconscious wish to return to the womb and the boundless feelings of bliss we all experienced in that state. This infantile desire reflects the anxious struggles of my ego to find balance and satisfaction in external reality, prompting a fearful wish to return to a safer time and place from earlier in life. (Such a wish is "pre-Oedipal" in reflecting a stage of psychological development that occurs prior to the Oedipal complex.) But the fulfillment of this wish is threatened by the rising pressures of the outside world, symbolized by the water, that defy my childish expectations and start forcing their way into my kitchen sanctuary.

The concerns about the L. story at the end of the dream express this basic wish in a more realistic and present-day context. While working on the project, I was relatively secluded and withdrawn from other activities; now the project is about to be "born" in published form, and I am anxious about leaving the pleasantly solitary, womb-like condition of the writing process and facing potential conflicts with other people in the external world.

Jung

From a Jungian perspective, the first step would be to amplify the dream's elements and images, seeking evidence of unconscious compensations for the imbalances of my conscious attitudes. The architectural imagery in the dream, somewhat like Jung's house dream (described in chapter 3), can be seen as a symbolic map of my intrapsychic condition. The backyard where I see the unfamiliar cats is a quieter and more secluded place than the front garden with Strauss and the dead bird. This physical arrangement of a private back and public front suggests the Jungian archetype of the persona, which represents the public identity we project in social situations, facing toward the outer world. Animals typically symbolize instinctual wishes and desires, according to Jung, and the prominence of cats in this dream opens up a host of possible amplifications: cats are widely respected and feared for their intelligence, independence, grace, and ferocity. They are both domesticated and wild, affectionate companions and bloodthirsty killers. The ancient Egyptians worshipped cats as companions of the gods, and European witches allegedly had cats as their animal familiars. These amplifications highlight a widespread belief in the mysterious spiritual powers of the feline race. At a subjective level of interpretation, the cats may express my own instincts and the challenge of domesticating their wildness.

Water has a wide range of possible symbolic meanings. In this instance, it might reflect unconscious emotions that have not been sufficiently expressed in waking life. The kitchen also has deep archetypal resonance as the primal center of family life, the warm hearth that gives protection and sustenance, a place where things are transformed (via cooking) from a wild form into something domesticated (edible food). By threatening to burst into the kitchen, the water prompts a different kind of transformation, from rigid enclosure to fluid expansion.

The dream might thus be a compensation for an unhealthy split in my personality, with too much separation between my outward-facing persona and my inward-facing true self. This split is also surfacing in my writing on the L. project, with rising anxiety about a possible gap between my private work and its public reception. By highlighting these conflicts and concerns, the dream is bringing new unconscious energies into waking awareness and thus promoting a stronger integration of all aspects of my personality.

Adler

An Adlerian approach would take this dream as a reflection of my efforts to defend my sense of superiority and self-worth. Looking at the associations to the dream, several events from waking life had shaken my sense of superiority. The concerns about mountain lions and trespassers, the statistics about global climate change, and the possibility of someone else writing about L.'s story all aggravated my feelings of vulnerability in the face of external events and situations I cannot control. The dream, in Adler's view, was formed in response to those waking-life difficulties, which my customary style of life had failed to manage effectively. The dream transformed my real problems into fantasy problems and thereby allowed me to use one of my customary strategies for defending against threats to my sense of superiority—the strategy of secluding myself from others and detaching from the external world, as I do in the dream when I go into the kitchen. This strategy is not very effective in dealing with my waking-life problems, but the dream alters the problem so that now the seclusion strategy will work (more or less). In Adlerian terms, the dream serves its function of preserving my sense of superiority and self-esteem, albeit without giving me any real help with the waking-life problem.

Boss

From Boss's existentialist perspective, dreams disclose aspects of our being-in-the-world, showing both unhealthy constrictions in our present life and stimulating potentials for our future. In this dream, the sensation of conflicted splitting is very strong. By focusing on the dream phenomenon itself, as Boss counsels, I see that the emotions of surprise, uncertainty, fear, and vulnerability are most prominent. The dream indicates that this split and conflicted mode of being-in-the-world is evident in many areas of my life (my public activities, my home life, my work). Boss would say that the dream is a real, genuine experience of being split—not a mere symbol or image, but an actual experience of that mode of being-in-the-world. However, the dream also reveals some genuine potentials for overcoming the splits and resolving the conflicts. The front and back yards are part of the same house; the kitchen décor integrates white and black; my wife's advice guides me toward better decisions. This suggests that through a full embrace of my being-in-the-world as disclosed in this dream, I can reach a more honest awareness of the fragmented aspects of my personality and see better ways to harmonize them in the future.

French and Fromm

The Ego Psychological approach of French and Fromm looks at every dream as an attempt by the ego to solve a pressing concern in waking life, what they term the focal conflict. In this dream, the focal conflict could be seen as the worries I have about lacking control in my various activities. I am afraid I can't keep the house and family together; can't preserve connections with the cherished past; can't stop trespassers, mountain lions, or global warming; can't keep inner emotions or outer pressures at bay; and can't stop other people from writing about things that I am writing about. My ego struggles mightily in the dream to master this focal conflict, with limited success. French and Fromm would sift through all my thoughts and activities in the dream and distinguish the ineffective efforts to deal with this conflict (e.g., remaining in the kitchen with the rising water outside) from efforts more likely to help me in the future (e.g., taking my wife's concerns more fully into account).

Perls

For Perls, dreams reveal holes in the Gestalt of our personalities, thereby confronting us with alienated, disowned parts of ourselves. In this dream, the most alienated elements seem to be the dead bird and the water outside the kitchen. By imaginatively identifying with the bird, as Perls recommends, I hear the bird say this: "I should be flying, free and unrestrained, but I have been killed by these cats. Their selfish instincts have ended my life. What a waste." By identifying with the water, I hear it say this: "I flow wherever gravity leads me, and nothing can block me forever. I can wash away anything; I am the universal solvent. Whatever gets in my way, I eventually push through it." Both the dead bird and the water occupy what Perls calls a psychological "underdog" position, in contrast to the superior "topdog" position of the cats and me in the kitchen. To follow Perls's method further, I would continue this dialogue with the dead bird and the water, bringing other elements from dream (such as the cats, the kitchen windows, my wife, and L.) into the conversation and trying to gain an understanding of the dream that includes and embraces all facets of the experience.

Hill

Hill's Cognitive-Experiential method uses a series of guided questions, following the exploration-insight-action sequence, to produce an interpretation that is both meaningful and useful to the dreamer. The exploration phase of working with my dream would cover much of the territory already covered in terms of associations to each element of the dream. The insight phase would also move in similar directions to the approaches of Jung, Boss, and French and Fromm in identifying a core concern about vulnerability, public interactions, and instinctual expression. Where Hill's method stands out from the others is its emphasis on an action phase, in which the exploration and insight prompt a plan for changes in waking life to put into practice the meanings learned from the dream. I can see several possible actions arising from the interpretation of this dream, one of which would be this: I should strive to learn more about the neighbors, fish, and mountain lions who are passing through our property and develop appropriate relations with each of them.

Aserinsky, Kleitman, Dement

Although I did not have this dream while attached to an EEG monitor in a sleep laboratory, it was almost certainly a dream experienced in REM sleep. The dream is fairly long, with lots of visual imagery, physical activity, and emotional involvement. I woke up in the morning with this dream fresh and vivid in my mind, so it seems probable that it came during the long REM period that for most humans occurs at the end of each night's sleep cycle.

Hobson

For Hobson, dreaming is activated by the random, chaotic neural activities of REM sleep. Higher mental functions then struggle to synthesize these bizarre inputs into a partly coherent sequence of images and events. My dream has several different settings and characters that seem only loosely related to each other. The emotions in the dream have obvious connections to my waking life, although in fairly trivial ways. It is true that I worry about cats, household order, and my professional work, but I knew that already. For Hobson there is no coded message here, no deep unconscious wisdom. The dream has simply responded to the random neural inputs of REM sleep by creating a semi-logical narrative that revolves around my ordinary waking concerns.

Solms

Solms does not identify dreaming with REM sleep, so his approach to the interpretation of a dream accepts the possibility that high-level cognitive processes are active in generating the feelings, themes, and images in the dreaming experience. However, Solms is otherwise in almost total agreement with Freud about the underlying operations of the human mind, so in the end, he would likely endorse a Freudian approach to my dream that emphasizes the fragility of my waking ego and the wish-fulfilling fantasy of returning to the safety and isolation of the womb.

Crick and Mitchison

The reverse-learning theory of Crick and Mitchison holds that REM sleep works to remove negative, parasitic modes of behavior from the brain. Following their theory, I should just forget my dream, because trying to remember and interpret it might preserve unhealthy patterns of thought that REM sleep is intended to eliminate.

Hall and Domhoff

Hall's quantitative approach would begin by analyzing this dream into its basic structural elements (including characters, social interactions, emotions, and settings). Briefly, a content analysis of this dream would include the following: the several cats, some familiar and some not; the dead bird; my wife; L., the historical figure; and the other people who might also write about her story. Although I perceive and think about many of these characters, there is only one social interaction in the dream that can be coded: a friendly interaction from my wife toward me, telling me to be careful. There are two clear instances of emotion in the dream: fear as the water gets into the kitchen and acute disappointment about someone else publishing L.'s story. The dream also includes two moments of apparent shock and confusion (trying to identify the bird, suddenly seeing the water coming into the kitchen), which might be not be coded by Hall's system unless the dream report explicitly mentions them. There are four settings: two outdoors and familiar (front and backyards of the old family house), one indoor and unfamiliar (the kitchen), and one with indeterminate location and familiarity (the part with the L. story). The objects mentioned in the dream are the walls, counters, and windows of the kitchen, and the water outside. After scoring the dream in this way, it could then be compared both to a longer series of my own dreams and to quantitative data on the dreams of other people. This would enable me to determine how often in my dreams I feel apprehension, how often cats appear, how many times I am threatened by water, and how often I have friendly interactions with my wife. At this point, it would be relatively easy to identify what Domhoff calls the "embodied simulations" of my waking-life concerns, which revolve around 1) the health and safety of my family and 2) people's future reactions to the L. project.

Foulkes

For Foulkes, dreams carry no specific message or intent to communicate. However, he says dreams are shaped by the same logical processes of order, coherence, and association that govern all thought. In my dream, evidence of such processes can be seen in the realistic portrayal of the front and backyards of our old house, the reasonable thoughts and reactions to the situation with the water coming into the kitchen, the accurate portrayal of my wife as a dispenser of sensible advice, and the honest assessment of how I would feel if someone else published an analysis of L.'s story before I do. These instances of normal, rational cognition demonstrate that no matter how bizarre dreams initially appear, on closer inspection it can usually be shown that they are shaped by the ordinary cognitive processes that psychologists have found operating in both waking and sleeping mentation.

Hunt

There are multiple types of dreams, according to Hunt, and each different type is formed by a different combination of cognitive processes. Although my dream does not fit easily into any of Hunt's categories (it has aspects of the personal-mnemonic, prophetic, archetypal-spiritual, and nightmare types), it does reflect the influence of both sophisticated grammatical structures and creative visual-spatial imagery. The grammatical structures can be seen in the coherence of each scene, with recognizable settings, plausible characters, and appropriate connections between perceptions, thoughts, and feelings. The creative visual-spatial imagery emerges with the significant shift from backyard to front yard, the sudden realization of water pressing in from outside the kitchen, and the uncanny sense that there is so much water it should already have broken into the kitchen. Hunt would likely view this image not as a bit of REM-generated nonsense with no meaningful connection to the rest of the dream, but rather as a vital visual-spatial image that enriches and intensifies the developing narrative thrust of the dream: the more I try to stay safe and isolated within the kitchen, the more dangerous elements from the outside press to get in.

Hartmann

I have had frequent nightmares for most of my life, though their occurrence has diminished in recent years. This dream has nightmarish qualities of shock, fear, and helplessness, although it does not have the classic form of a chase or attack nightmare. Hartmann's theory that people with frequent nightmares have thin psychological boundaries is relevant for my life in various ways; although I have not taken his diagnostic test, I am certainly on the thin-boundary end of the spectrum. Having thin boundaries makes one vulnerable to many kinds of threats, which can give rise to frightening dreams. Looking at the nightmarish qualities of this particular dream, many of the actions and emotions revolve around threats to boundaries. The unfamiliar cats entering my backyard, the water seeping into the kitchen, and the other people writing about L.'s story—in each case I am concerned about a boundary being violated. My dream takes advantage of the "looser connections" in the sleeping mind to bring together several areas of my life that seem separate but are actually united in highlighting a deep concern about protecting my psychological boundaries.

Popular Psychologists

Popular psychologists like Faraday, Garfield, Delaney, Ullman, Taylor, and LaBerge offer a variety of practical techniques for exploring a dream's meaning. To start, they recommend carefully studying each image in the dream. For example, using Delaney's "pretend I'm from another planet" method, I would describe a backyard as a place for people to relax at home in privacy and cats as animals with a close but ambivalent relationship with humans. I would then use these insights to build bridges between the dream and my waking life (for instance, by identifying a feeling of ambivalence about being able to relax the way I used to). Popular psychologists would also recommend I try to incubate a future dream to gain additional insights into this one (e.g., by going to sleep repeating the phrase, "How can I become more comfortable with these new cats in my old home?"). They would also encourage me to try to become lucid, so I could confront threatening forces like the water outside the kitchen and try to find a better, less conflicted way of interacting with them. Finally, popular psychologists would prompt me to share this dream with other people and seek their comments and reflections. Using Taylor's "if it were *my* dream" method, I would ask different people to project their thoughts and feelings onto my dream, eliciting their intuitive responses to themes that are rooted in collective human concerns.

Summary

Such an exercise in comparative dream analysis cannot, of course, do full justice to any of the individual theories. For instance, a complete Jungian interpretation would require a far more detailed probing of the dreamer's personal life and a much broader amplification of the dream's archetypal symbolism than I have provided. An adequate content analysis using the Hall and Van de Castle system would demand the careful scoring of a long series of my dreams. An assessment using the theories of Hobson or Foulkes would need extensive data from the sleep laboratory before offering any conclusions. These are complex and sophisticated models, and their greatest benefits only emerge when they are applied in a very thorough and systematic fashion. But the primary goal of the above exercise has been a modest one—namely, to give readers a concrete illustration of how the different psychological theories presented in this book would be used to interpret and explain a sample dream.

Major Areas of Debate

A second goal of this comparative dream analysis is to highlight the major areas of debate among psychological theories of dreaming. Despite, or perhaps because of, more than 100 years of concentrated study, modern psychologists disagree on many fundamental points about the formation, function, and interpretation of dreams.

Formation

There are at least three major debates regarding the formation of dreams. First, what is the nature of the unconscious forces that work to form our dreams? Are these forces dark and destructive (Freud), or are they positive, creative, and even spiritual in nature (Jung)? Second, can dream formation be explained without using the imprecise notion of "the unconscious"? Many psychologists (Adler, Boss, Piaget, Hall) argue that a better explanation of dream formation refers to those same basic structures of personality and cognition that operate in our waking lives. Third, what is the role of REM-sleep physiology in the formation of dreams? Some researchers (Hobson, Crick and Mitchison) assert that the neural activities of REM sleep dominate the process of dream formation, while other psychologists (Foulkes, Hartmann, Hunt, LaBerge) see a complex interaction of REM physiology and cognitive-emotional forces at work in the formation of dreams.

Function

There are at least four major positions on the question of what function dreams serve. The first position (Freud, Adler) is that dreams function to deceive consciousness, masking unpleasant truths and thereby preserving our customary psychological defenses. The second position (Jung, Boss, French and Fromm, Perls, Hartmann, Hunt, all popular psychologists) is that dreams serve a variety of highly positive functions: giving deep insights into neglected thoughts and emotions, helping solve important problems in daily life, stimulating creativity and imagination, and promoting the overall integration of personality. The third position (Hall, Domhoff, Foulkes) is that dreams have little or no psychological function beyond a modest value in diagnosing psychological disturbances. The fourth position (Hobson, Crick and Mitchison) is that the real functions are served not by dreaming but by REM sleep, in its role of providing routine maintenance of basic neurological circuitry in the brain.

Interpretation

Those who see no psychological function to dreams naturally have little interest in trying to interpret dreams. Those who do believe that dreams serve some psychological function approach the process of interpretation from a number of different directions. Most psychologists (following Freud) insist that any dream interpretation must begin with the personal associations of the dreamer. Some (like Jung) also seek amplifications to the dream's images and symbols. However, others (like Boss) reject associations and amplifications and say that interpretation should focus exclusively on the dreamer's experience itself. Still others (like Hall) argue that even the dreamer is unnecessary because nothing more than a series of written dream reports is required to make valid interpretations.

Many psychologists (Freud, Jung, Adler, Boss, French and Fromm) regard the aid of a trained psychotherapist as a valuable or even essential part of dream interpretation. Others (Hill, Hall, Faraday, Garfield, Delaney) disagree, saying that with a little practice any person can learn to interpret his or her own dreams. And for some (Perls, Ullman, Taylor), the ideal setting for dream interpretation is neither one-to-one psychotherapy nor private reflection and journal writing, but a dream-sharing group. Finally, some psychologists (Freud, Hall) argue that dream interpretation can be precise, objective, and scientific in its results. Most psychologists, however, believe that dream interpretation is more of an intuitive art in which many complex and multivalent meanings emerge out of each dream.

Modern Psychology's Answers in the Context of Western History

As a final way of evaluating the answers given by modern psychologists to the three basic questions, they may be compared to the answers given earlier in Western history to the same questions.

The Bible

A number of modern psychologists (Jung, Boss, Hunt) basically agree with the Bible that at least some of our dreams are formed by God or by other divine, supernatural, or transpersonal forces. The theories of these psychologists also correspond closely to the Bible's portrayal of dream functions as providing spiritual revelations, prophecies, and warnings of possible danger relevant to individuals and the broader community. And almost all psychologists agree with the Bible that while the best dream interpretations are guided by a kind of intuitive inspiration, it is very easy to misinterpret dreams if we are not careful in our analyses and reflections.

Aristotle

A large number of modern psychologists, perhaps the majority, follow Aristotle (and the skeptical voices in the Bible) in arguing that dreams are formed by the dreamer's own sleeping mind. Aristotle's rationalistic view that dreams have no specific function is mirrored in the theories of many psychologists (Hobson, Crick and Mitchison, Foulkes, Domhoff). But Aristotle grants that dreams, while not intentional messages from the gods, may still be read for useful information about the dreamer's life. His dictum that becoming a skillful interpreter of dreams requires learning how to use the "faculty of observing resemblances" could be taken as the cardinal law of all modern psychological dream interpretation from Freud onward.

Artemidorus

Echoes of Artemidorus, particularly his thoughts about the function and interpretation of dreams, can be heard in the theories of many modern psychologists (Freud, Jung, Hall). But the approach of Artemidorus is most closely related to the work of popular psychologists. He shares with them a disinclination to engage in theological debates about where dreams come from, a deep interest in dreams as bearing messages that can be used to improve the waking lives of ordinary people, a method of carefully examining the dreamer's personal life, and a reliance on one's own experience and native intelligence to guide the process of interpretation. In all these ways, Artemidorus anticipates the attitudes, approaches, and techniques of popular psychologists.

It is beyond the scope of this book to examine in any further detail these historical influences and connections. My hope, however, is that readers will themselves go on to study the historical predecessors to the dream theories of modern psychologists (and, beyond that, to investigate the cross-cultural parallels to and variations from these theories). Because dreaming is both an intimate personal experience and a phenomenon found in all cultures and eras of history, it offers a wonderful pathway for people to explore and celebrate the shared yet infinitely varied humanity that unites every one of us.

The Sleep and Dream Database: A Practical Guide to Digitally Enhanced Dream Research

Introduction

This appendix describes the functions of the Sleep and Dream Database (SDDb), a searchable digital archive designed to promote a data-driven approach to dream research. The contents and tools of the SDDb enable users to apply basic technologies of data analysis to observe and identify the meaningful dimensions of dreaming experience. The goal of this kind of research is not to replace other modes of interpretation and analysis, but rather to enrich them with new insights into the recurrent patterns of dream content. Anyone who studies dreams, from whatever perspective and for whatever purpose, can benefit from more knowledge about these patterns.

The SDDb is not the only online resource for this kind of approach to the study of dreams. The DreamBank.net website run by G. William Domhoff and Adam Schneider also has a large online collection of dream reports gathered by various researchers that can be searched and analyzed in many ways. The future will likely witness the development of many other online databases with valuable collections of dream material. The following discussion will focus on the SDDb as a case study in order to highlight some of the principles involved in digitally enhanced dream research.

The SDDb currently contains more than 25,000 dream reports of various types from a wide range of people. Some of the reports come from individuals who have kept a dream journal for many years. Some of the reports come from participants who filled out surveys and questionnaires. Some come from the studies of other researchers who have generously shared their experimental data with me. The SDDb also includes dream reports from anthropological studies, historical texts, literary sources, and media interviews. (The database does not, however, contain dream reports that users have entered directly through an online portal. In other words, the SDDb cannot currently be used as an online dream journaling system. That feature awaits future development.)

The SDDb also includes, in addition to dream reports, the answers given by survey participants to a variety of questions about their sleep and dreaming, for example how often they remember their dreams, how often they experience insomnia, have they ever had a dream of flying or lucid dreaming, etc. The data also include people's responses to various demographic questions about their gender, age, race/ethnicity, education, religious practices, political beliefs, etc.

This combination of a large number of narrative dream reports plus a large amount of quantitative survey data makes the SDDb an especially useful resource for the study of dreaming.

The SDDb offers two basic functions for exploring this material. One, "Survey Analysis," enables users to compare people's answers to questions posed on a survey or questionnaire. This function enables you to create a statistical table to compare, for example, the dream recall frequencies of people from different age groups or the insomnia frequencies of people with different political views or the occurrence of lucid dreams among men and women.

The other function, "Word Searching," enables users to sift through large numbers of dreams for particular words and phrases. You can search the dreams by choosing your own word strings, and/or you can also use the built-in word search templates to search for typical categories of dream content. This function allows you, for example, to choose a particular set of dreams and search it for all the references to water or colors or emotions or the names of famous people or places.

The development of the SDDb began in the early 2000s in consultation with G. William Domhoff and Adam Schneider, who helped me understand how to use their DreamBank.net website. With their encouragement, I started designing a new, complementary database that would 1) include both dream reports and survey data, 2) allow for the easy use of built-in word search templates, and 3) have enough flexibility to enable a wide range of searches and analyses. In 2009 I worked with Kurt Bollacker, a software designer and engineer, to build the first version of the database. In 2014 I began working with GRAYBOX, a web technology company, to expand the scope of the SDDb and improve its user interface. The SDDb will always be a work in progress, but the basic functionality is in place, and it has already supported two doctoral dissertation projects, by Mary Walsh (Walsh 2014) and Robert Sears (Sears 2015), and a recent book (Bulkeley 2016).

The major advantages of the word search function as a mode of dream research include its speed, transparency, replicability, flexibility, and power to analyze very large quantities of material. The process is fairly easy to learn, and sites like the SDDb and DreamBank.net provide free and open access for users to engage in their own study projects aided by these new digital tools.

The major disadvantages of this approach should also be noted. They include deemphasizing the qualitative aspects of dreaming, overemphasizing the measurability of dream content, and leaving open the key question of how to connect the numerical frequencies of word usage with the waking-life concerns of the dreamer.

These disadvantages can be diminished to a degree by using quantitative analysis as one method among many others in a multidisciplinary approach to dreams. There is no reason in principle why word-search methods cannot work in coordination with other methods using qualitative insights and evaluations. Indeed, I believe the future prosperity of dream research depends on developing better interdisciplinary models for integrating the results of several different methods of study. The users of the SDDb can make important progress in creating those models.

To address the challenge of how to connect the word-usage frequencies with relevant aspects of the dreamer's life, I advise users to keep two principles in mind. These principles suggest paths for exploring the potentially meaningful connections between the dreams and the individual's waking situation.

One principle is the *continuity hypothesis*: the relative frequency with which something appears in a person's dreams can be a reflection of its importance as a meaningful concern in the person's waking life. In other words, the more often something (a character, setting, activity) shows up in dreams, the more emotionally important it's likely to be in waking life.

The other principle is the *discontinuity hypothesis*: infrequent and anomalous elements of dream content can be spontaneous expressions of playful imagination, occurring at any point in life but especially in times of crisis, change, or transition. Something that appears very rarely and is dramatically discontinuous with typical patterns of dream content can reflect the mind's concerted effort to go beyond what *is* to imagine what *might be*.

The continuity hypothesis has an enormous amount of research literature supporting its basic tenets (as discussed in chapter 6). Its usefulness has been well established for many years. The discontinuity hypothesis, by contrast, is more recent, harder to study and analyze, and more theoretically than empirically grounded (drawing on Jung and Hunt among others), but potentially useful, too, in giving users a practical way of thinking about the symbolic and metaphorical dimensions of dreaming.

Survey Analysis

The Survey Analysis function lets you compare the answers that different groups of people give to questions about their sleep and dreams. This tool lets you create statistical tables that focus on whatever demographic variables you want to study.

The SDDb currently includes results from ten different surveys I designed and commissioned to study sleep and dream patterns among contemporary Americans. The field research for these surveys was conducted by a number different opinion research companies (Zogby Analytics, Harris Interactive, You.Gov), all but one of which administered the surveys online (one, by Quinlan Greenberg Rosner Research, was performed by random-digit telephone dialing).

More surveys will be added to the database, but this initial collection includes responses from more than 15,000 participants. All of the surveys include responses to questions about demographics (age, gender, region of residence, etc.) along with questions about sleep and dreams (frequency of insomnia, dream recall, sharing dreams with others, etc.). Most of the surveys also include questions asking for a narrative report of a dream (e.g., a lucid dream, a nightmare, a highly memorable dream), and many of the surveys include demographic questions about religion and politics.

An important point to note is that many of the surveys posed slightly different questions and answer categories for the same general topic. This means that SDDb users need to look closely at the results of any comparison to see which surveys are being included in the results. (This information is presented at the bottom of every Survey Analysis Results page.)

Here is an example of the kind of inquiry that can be easily performed using the SDDb. Let's start with the two most important variables that have been studied in relation to dream recall, namely gender and age. How does a person's gender and age correlate with the frequency of his or her dream recall? We can gain helpful empirical insights into that question by the following analyses.

First, we choose one of the surveys available for study in the Survey Analysis page's menu. Several surveys could serve as examples; let's look at the 2015 Demographic Survey, which includes responses from 2,303 participants.

Then we choose the questions of comparison. If we make a table comparing people's answers to questions of gender and dream recall, we find that women remember slightly more dreams than men do. Summarizing the results (i.e., combining the frequencies of people who answered "almost every morning or more often," "several times a week," and "once a week") and rounding to the nearest whole number, 56 percent of the women remembered a dream once a week or more often, compared to 52 percent of the men who remembered their dreams this often.

Next, we try a new analysis with the same survey, comparing participants' ages to their dream recall. For this analysis, we use the variable "Age Group D," which divides the participants into three age groupings (18–34, 35–54, 55+). The results show that younger people remember dreams much more frequently than do older people. For the youngest age group, 64 percent reported remembering their dreams once a week or more, while 55 percent of the middle-age group and 49 percent of the oldest age group said they remembered their dreams this often.

The SDDb enables users to pursue the analysis further than this. We might wonder, do men and women remember their dreams with similar frequencies at the same ages? Do young men remember more dreams than old men, and young women more than old women?

This kind of analysis can be performed by using the constraints feature. After choosing to make a table comparing the questions for Age Group D and dream recall, we can add a constraint by selecting the gender question and choosing either male or female participants. By doing this we filter the analysis so we only see results for that specific subset of participants. Starting with the males as a constraint, we find that the 18–34 group does not have significantly more dream recall than the 55+ group (55 percent versus 51 percent). But when we use the females as a constraint, the results differ more dramatically, with 69 percent of the 18–34 group remembering their dreams once a week or more, while only 47 percent of the 55+ remembered their dreams that often.

These results can be taken as evidence that men's dream-recall frequency is more consistent over their life span, and women's recall frequency is more variable, with an especially high rate in early life and a considerable drop thereafter.

This example has shown that with nothing more than a few computer clicks, we are able to identify an intriguing pattern in dream-recall frequency among men and women of different ages. We have to be careful, however, because even though a sizable number of people participated in this survey, their answers may not be representative of all of humankind, so we should not overgeneralize about the significance of such results. I believe it is vital to remain humble in this kind of research, in recognition of the wide variability of dreaming experience among the general human population.

To determine if this pattern is true only of the participants in this survey or applies to other people as well, we could try a similar search process using other surveys in the SDDb. We could also look at age and gender variations in relation to other demographic categories like race/ethnicity, education, income, religious activities, and political views. There may be other variables at play that need to be considered before reaching any settled conclusions.

The Survey Analysis function can be applied to the study of a wide range of topics, with the capacity for even more finely grained investigations. For example, if you wanted to compare the dream-recall frequency of younger versus older women, all of whom who graduated from four-year colleges, describe themselves as politically conservative, and live in the American south, then you could create a table using those variables and constraints. You would then learn that 67 percent of the younger women with all these attributes remember their dreams once a week or more, while only 14 percent of the older women remember their dreams that frequently.

Using more constraints in an analysis leads to a smaller number of participants who fit the criteria, making the statistical frequencies of the results shakier and more subject to chance. (In the comparison above, there were only six women in the younger group and seven in the older group.) Here as elsewhere, caution and modesty are advised in drawing appropriate conclusions from the results of your analyses.

Word Searching

The Word Searching function has even greater range and flexibility than the Survey Analysis function. This function enables you to sift through large numbers of dream reports for particular words and phrases. The SDDb automatically calculates the percentage of dreams in which the selected word or phrase appears at least once. This percentage allows users to compare patterns of word usage in various kinds of dreams from various kinds of people.

The Word Searching process begins with the selection of a source of dream reports. The SDDb contains reports from many different sources, including personal journals, questionnaires, psychology experiments, anthropological studies, and media interviews among others. The first choice to make in using this function is which dreams to explore. As a simple introductory demonstration, let's just select "All Surveys," which will draw on all the sources in the SDDb. Next, we choose a constraint, which is optional but allows for more focused results. Again, to keep it simple, we can choose "males" from the constraint menu for the "gender" question.

Next is a choice of the type of dream report to be searched. The dreams in the SDDb have been provided in response to several kinds of questions. Examples include, what is your most recent dream? What is your most memorable dream? What is your worst nightmare? Have you ever had a visitation dream (in which someone who is dead appears as if alive)? Each different type of dream has special qualities and is worthy of detailed study, which the SDDb makes relatively easy to do. For this initial search, we can select "Most Recent Dream" as the type of dream text.

The next step is an important one, regarding the length of the dream reports to be searched. The SDDb allows users to set a minimum and maximum word length for the dream reports to be searched. For most kinds of study, this feature is highly recommended. Some of the responses in the SDDb are not dreams *per se*—they may be people saying, "I don't know" or "Can't remember" or sometimes colorful rebukes for my audacity in asking the question! Rather than removing those responses, I usually screen them out by choosing a minimum word length, usually 10 or 25 words. That means the search will not include many genuine dream reports of shorter length. For some studies, that might be a drawback, but not in ours, for which I'm setting a minimum length of 25 words and a maximum of 300 words.

Then comes the last step, choosing the word or words to search in the set of dreams we have just defined. The easiest way to get interesting results is to use the SDDb templates for word searching, with versions 1.0 and 2.0 built into the website. The 2.0 version has 40 categories of content grouped into eight classes of dream content: Perception, Emotion, Cognition, Natural Elements, Movement, Characters, Social Interactions, and Culture. Each of the 40 categories is comprised of dozens of words relating to that topic. These categories are not drawn from a generic coding scheme unrelated to dream research, but have been developed over time as a direct continuation of the system devised by Calvin Hall and Robert Van de Castle and refined by G. William Domhoff and Adam Schneider to empirically study dream content. In this way, the SDDb templates provide an approach to digital dream research that is backward-compatible with pre-digital methods of study. I believe this is a key methodological principle: as we move into the technologically enhanced future of studying dreams, we should make sure to integrate new findings with the hard-won knowledge of the past.

From the 2.0 template menu, let's select one of the emotions, the category for "Fear." In the version of the database available as I write, this search shows 1,667 dream reports that fit the search criteria (from males in all sources, in most recent dream texts of 25–300 words in length). Of these, 266 have at least one reference to a word in the "Fear" category, a total (rounded to the nearest whole number) of 16 percent.

The Results page shows in the left column the frequency of usage for each of the words in the category. In this case, the four most used words in these dreams were *scared*, *afraid*, *fear*, and *frightened*. In the right column, the dream reports themselves appear, with the word(s) from the selected category highlighted.

To be clear, these results show *every* use of the words in the selected category. The results may include references to fear that do not have to do with the dreamer's emotional state. The results may include uses of the term that are metaphorical or fictional or incidental. (If desired, users can perform an additional screening process to remove dream reports from the search that are judged irrelevant to the primary search.)

For a general inquiry like this one, we can take the unfiltered results as a rough measure of the incidence of fear in men's dreams. To take the process a step further, we can perform the same search while changing the constraint from "male" to "female." Here the Results page shows that out of the 1,984 dream reports that fit the search criteria (from females in all sources, in most recent dream texts of 25–300 words in length), 437 have at least one reference to a word in the "Fear" category, a total of 22 percent. The four most used words from the category were *scared*, *afraid*, *upset*, and *fear*.

These findings can be taken as evidence suggesting that women's dreams have considerably more references to fear than do men's dreams. However, as with all studies using the tools of the SDDb, caution is needed in the interpretation of the results of any word search. Many more studies would have to be performed, and other research findings consulted, before making a firm statement about a broad topic like fear in men's and women's dreams.

The findings of one search often lead to new questions requiring new searches. For instance, we can extend this line of inquiry by asking if the gender difference in fear references also appears in children's dreams. The SDDb includes a set of dreams gathered from children ages 8 to 18 via an online survey administered by Harris Interactive in 2011. The participants were asked to describe their "most memorable" dreams, which are different from most recent dreams in favoring unusual and emotionally intense types of dream content. The comparison is not perfect, but in this inquiry, we are exploring a general trend, and we can refine the analysis at later stages if desired.

Using the same search parameters (reports of 25–300 words in length), the results show that for the boys, 37 of the 205 dream reports, or 18 percent, contained at least one reference to fear, with the four most used words being *scared, nervous, afraid,* and *scare.* For the girls, 80 of the 372 dreams, or 22 percent, contained at least one reference to fear, with the four most used words being *scared, terrified, afraid,* and *fear.* This is still a difference, but not as big as with the adult most recent dreams.

This line of investigation could continue from here in any of several different directions. But let's turn to a different kind of word search strategy, one that can yield more personally relevant kinds of insights. The SDDb includes several lengthy series of dreams from individuals who recorded their dreams on a regular basis for an extended period, in some cases covering many years. The study of the patterns in these dream reports can often lead to the discovery (guided by the continuity and discontinuity hypotheses) of meaningful connections between the dreams and the individual's waking-life concerns.

To illustrate how this kind of search process works, let's select "Nan Journal 2001-2002" from the menu. Clicking the search button at this point will show all 26 dream reports in her series, which range in length from 12 to 397 words, with a median length of 116 words (meaning half the dreams are longer than, and half the dreams shorter than, 116 words). This is one of the shortest series in the SDDb, but it is a good one for quickly illustrating what can be learned with word search methods.

Nan (not her real name) kept a journal of her dreams for six months following a nearly fatal car crash, while she recuperated in a hospital. You would not know about the crash from the dreams themselves, which never directly refer to it. This highlights a crucial finding of dream research: the patterns of dream content reflect people's waking *concerns,* not necessarily their waking activities or behavior. Nan dreamed not about the car crash, but about its emotional and interpersonal implications.

In Nan's case, her dreams indicate she definitely did feel strong concerns at this time, in a mostly negative direction. Of her 26 dreams, 8 of them (31 percent) have at least one reference to fear. There are also five references to death (19 percent), six to physical aggression (23 percent), and none to happiness. These frequencies accurately reflect the frightened and vulnerable quality of Nan's feelings in waking life.

Looking more closely at the characters in her dreams, a man named Phil appears in 6 of the dreams (23 percent), more than any other character in the series. Following the continuity hypothesis, we can infer that Phil is a person of great concern to her, and this turns out to be true. Phil is Nan's ex-husband. She had divorced him 10 years earlier, after which she started an independent career as an art teacher. After the accident, she recuperated in a hospital ward with several other women, all much older than Nan, all of whom had severe mobility problems. The sad plight of these women stoked Nan's fears and raised the darkest concern in her life: she might have to return to Phil and become reliant on him again. Her dreams accurately reflected her strongly negative feelings about the possibility of Phil becoming more of a presence again in her waking life.

Nan's waking-life interests in art are also reflected in her dreams, and one dream in particular made an especially strong psychological impact on her. This dream features a magical paintbrush painting a beautiful rainbow pattern on the walls of her childhood home. It is the only dream in the series with so many colors, the only one with a magical object, and one of only two dreams in which she describes something as "beautiful." Following the discontinuity hypothesis, we can infer that an unusually creative and playful dream like this would prompt Nan to think beyond what *is* to imagine what *might be*, and that does seem to have been the case. She told me she regarded this dream as a reassuring sign of hope and healing in her long, dark road to physical and mental recovery. Like the first green shoots of spring, Nan's "bizarre" dream of the magical paintbrush heralded the eventual return of color, beauty, and creative vitality in her waking life.

Other series in the SDDb have many more dreams covering much longer periods of time. As a general principle, the longer the series of dreams, the stronger the results of analyzing those dreams. Although even a short series like Nan's can yield valuable findings, the potential for meaningful insights and discoveries is greatest with a long series of dreams. The SDDb currently has several series of 100 or more dream reports, including those of Brianna, Bea, Magnolia, Beverly, Jordan, Lawrence, KB, KM, Mike, BS, the Natural Scientist, and Jasmine (all pseudonyms), with more on the way.

Experience is the best teacher, so I encourage users to play with the SDDb and other databases like it, experiment with different kinds of searches and analyses, and think carefully about how the results relate to other insights that researchers from various fields have gained about the nature and meaning of dreams. Good luck, and let me know how it goes!

Bibliography

Note: Good general resources for information on current research on the psychology of dreaming include:

1. the IASD journal *Dreaming*, published quarterly by the American Psychological Association;
2. *The Encyclopedia of Sleep and Dreaming*, ed. Mary Carskadon (1993);
3. the volumes in the *Series in Dream Studies* from State University of New York Press, ed. Robert Van de Castle (1991–2011);
4. the three-volume set *The New Science of Dreaming*, eds. Deirdre Barrett and Patrick McNamara (2007);
5. *Dreams: Biology, Psychology, and Culture*, eds. Katja Valli, Robert Hoss, and Robert Gongloff (2017).

Several of the references included in the bibliography below are not directly mentioned in the text, but are potentially useful for readers interested in further study in the psychology of dreaming.

Adler, Alfred. 1956. *The Individual Psychology of Alfred Adler*. Edited by H. L. Ansbacher and R. R. Ansbacher. New York: Harper Torchbooks.

Adler, Shelley. 2011. *Sleep Paralysis: Night-Mares, Nocebos, and the Mind-Body Connection*. New Brunswick: Rutgers University Press.

Aizenstat, Stephen and Robert Bosnak, eds. 2009. *Imagination and Medicine*. New Orleans: Spring.

Alston, T., R. Calogeras, and H. Deserno, eds. 1993. *Dream Reader: Psychoanalytic Articles on Dreams*. New York: International Universities Press.

Antrobus, John. 1993. "Dreaming: Could We Do Without It?" In *The Functions of Dreaming*, edited by Alan Moffitt, Milton Kramer, and Robert Hoffmann. Albany: State University of New York Press.

Arber, Sara, Marcos Bote, and Robert Meadows. 2009. "Gender and Socio-economic Patterning of Self-Reported Sleep Problems in Britain." *Social Science & Medicine* 68: 281–289.

Arber, Sara, Robert Meadows, and S. Venn. 2012. "Sleep and Society." In *The Oxford Handbook of Sleep and Sleep Disorders*, edited by Charles Morin and Colin Espie, 223–247. New York: Oxford University Press.

Aristides, Aelius. 1981. *The Complete Works*. Translated by Charles Behr. Leiden: E.J. Brill.

Aristotle. 1941a. "On Dreams." In *The Collected Works of Aristotle*, edited by R. McKeon. New York: Random House.

Aristotle. 1941b. "On Prophesying by Dreams." In *The Collected Works of Aristotle*, edited by R. McKeon. New York: Random House.

Armitage, R. 1992. "Gender Differences and the Effect of Stress on Dream Recall: A 30-Day Diary Report." *Dreaming* 2: 137–142.

Artemidorus. 1975. *The Interpretation of Dreams*. Translated by Robert White. Park Ridge, NJ: Noyes Press.

Aserinsky, Eugene, and Nathaniel Kleitman. 1953. "Regularly Occurring Periods of Eye Motility, and Concomitant Phenomena, during Sleep." *Science* 118: 273–274.

Aserinsky, Eugene, and Nathaniel Kleitman. 1955. "Two Types of Ocular Motility Occurring in Sleep." *Journal of Applied Physiology* 8: 1–10.

Aydar, Hidayet. 2009. "*Istikhara* and Dreams: Learning about the Future through Dreaming." In *Dreaming in Christianity and Islam: Culture, Conflict, and Creativity*, edited by Kelly Bulkeley, Kate Adams, and Patricia Davis, 123–136. New Brunswick: Rutgers University Press.

Baars, B. and W. Banks. 1994. "Dream Consciousness: A Neurocognitive Approach." *Consciousness and Cognition* 3.

Bakan, David. 1958. *Sigmund Freud and the Jewish Mystical Tradition*. Boston: Beacon Press.

Barrett, Deirdre. 1991. "Flying Dreams and Lucidity: An Empirical Study of Their Relationship." *Dreaming* 1: 129–134.

Barrett, Deirdre. 1992. "Just How Lucid Are Lucid Dreams?" *Dreaming* 2: 221–228.

Barrett, Deirdre. 1994. "Dreams in Dissociative Disorders." *Dreaming* 4: 165–176.

Barrett, Deirdre, ed. 1996. *Trauma and Dreams*. Cambridge: Harvard University Press.

Bearden, C. 1994. "The Nightmare: Biological and Psychological Origins." *Dreaming* 4: 139–152.

Beaudet, Denyse. 1990. *Encountering the Monster: Pathways in Children's Dreams*. New York: Continuum.

Beaulieu-Prevost, Dominic and Antonio Zadra. 2005. "Dream Recall Frequency and Attitude towards Dreams: A Reinterpretation of the Relation." *Personality and Individual Differences* 38: 919–927.

Beaulieu-Prevost, Dominic and Antonio Zadra. 2007. "Absorption, Psychological Boundaries and Attitude towards Dreams as Correlates of Dream Recall: Two Decades of Research Seen through a Meta-Analysis." *Journal of Sleep Research* 16: 51–59.

Belicki, Kathryne. 1987. "Recalling Dreams: An Examination of Daily Variation and Individual Differences." In *Sleep and Dreams: A Sourcebook*, edited by Jayne Gackenbach, 187–206. New York: Garland Publishing.

Bell, A. and Calvin Hall. 1971. *The Personality of a Child Molester: An Analysis of Dreams*. Chicago: Aldine Atherton.

Beradt, Charlotte. 1996. *The Third Reich of Dreams*. Translated by A. Gottwald. Chicago: Quadrangle Books.

Berne, P. and L. Savary. 1991. *Dream Symbol Work*. Mahwah: Paulist Press.

Bernheimer, C. and C. Kahane, eds. 1985. *In Dora's Case: Freud-Hysteria-Feminism*. New York: Columbia University Press.

Binswanger, Ludwig. 1967. *Being in the World: Selected Papers of Ludwig Binswanger*. Translated by Jacob Needleman. New York: Harper Torchbooks.

Binswanger, Ludwig. 1993. "Dream and Existence." In *Dream and Existence*, edited by K. Hoeller. Atlantic Highlands, NJ: Humanities Press.

Blagrove, Mark. 1992. "Dreams as the Reflection of Our Waking Concerns and Abilities: A Critique of the Problem-Solving Paradigm in Dream Research." *Dreaming* 2: 205–220.

Bogzaran, Fariba and Daniel Deslauriers. 2012. *Integral Dreaming: A Holistic Approach to Dreams*. Albany: State University of New York Press.

Bonime, Walter, with F. Bonime. 1988. *The Clinical Use of Dreams*. New York: DeCapo Press.

Bosnak, Robert. 1988. *A Little Course in Dreams*. Boston: Shambhala.

Bosnak, Robert. 1989. *Dreaming with an AIDS Patient: An Intimate Look inside the Dreams of a Gay Man with AIDS by His Analyst*. Boston: Shambhala.

Bosnak, Robert. 1996. *Tracks in the Wilderness of Dreaming: Exploring Interior Landscape through Practical Dreamwork*. New York: Delacorte Press.

Boss, Medard. 1958. *The Analysis of Dreams*. New York: Philosophical Library.

Boss, Medard. 1977. *I Dreamt Last Night . . .* New York: Gardner.

Braun, A. R., T. J. Balkin, N. J. Wesensten, F. Gwadry, R. E. Carson, M. Varga, P. Baldwin, G. Belenky, and P. Herscovitch. 1998. "Dissociated Pattern of Activity in Visual Cortices and Their Projections during Human Rapid Eye-Movement Sleep." *Science* 279: 91–95.

Brenneis, C. 1975. "Developmental Aspects of Aging in Women: A Comparative Study of Dreams." *Archives of General Psychiatry* 32: 429–434.

Brockway, S. S. 1987. "Group Treatment of Combat Nightmares in Post-Traumatic Stress Disorder." *Journal of Contemporary Psychotherapy* 17: 270–284.

Brooks, S., ed. 1987. *The Oxford Book of Dreams*. Oxford: Oxford University Press.

Buckner, Randy L., Jessica R. Andrews-Hanna, and Daniel L. Schachter. 2008. "The Brain's Default Network: Anatomy, Function, and Relevance to Disease." *Annals of the New York Academy of Sciences* 1124: 1–38.

Bulkeley, Kelly. 1993. "Dreaming Is Play." *Psychoanalytic Psychology* 10: 501–514.

Bulkeley, Kelly. 2008. *Dreaming in the World's Religions: A Comparative History.* New York: New York University Press.

Bulkeley, Kelly. 2008. *American Dreamers.* Boston: Beacon Press.

Bulkeley, Kelly. 2012. "Dream Recall and Political Ideology: Results of a Demographic Survey." *Dreaming* 22: 1–9.

Bulkeley, Kelly. 2012. "Dreaming in Adolescence: A 'Blind' Word Search of a Teenage Girl's Dream Series." *Dreaming* 22: 240–252.

Bulkeley, Kelly. 2014. "Lucid Dreaming by the Numbers." In *Lucid Dreaming: New Perspectives on Consciousness in Sleep,* edited by Ryan Hurd and Kelly Bulkeley, 1–22. Santa Barbara, CA: ABC-CLIO.

Bulkeley, Kelly and G. William Domhoff. 2010. "Detecting Meaning in Dream Reports: An Extension of a Word Search Approach." *Dreaming* 20: 77–95.

Bulkeley, Kelly and Ryan Hurd. 2014. "Introduction." In *Lucid Dreaming: New Perspectives on Consciousness in Sleep,* vol. 1, edited by Ryan Hurd and Kelly Bulkeley, xiii–xxxii. Santa Barbara, CA: ABC-CLIO.

Bynum, Edward Bruce. 1993. *Families and the Interpretation of Dreams: Awakening the Intimate Web.* New York: Harrington Park Press.

Calkins, Mary. 1893. "Statistics of Dreams." *The American Journal of Psychology* 5: 311–343.

Cartwright, Rosalind. 1979. *Night Life: Explorations in Dreaming.* Englewood Cliffs, NJ: Prentice-Hall.

Cartwright, Rosalind. 1991. "Dreams That Work: The Relation of Dream Incorporation to Adaptation to Stressful Events." *Dreaming* 1: 3–10.

Cartwright, Rosalind. 1993. "Who Needs Their Dreams? The Usefulness of Dreams in Psychotherapy." *Journal of the American Academy of Psychoanalysis* 21: 539–547.

Cartwright, Rosalind. 2010. *The 24-Hour Mind: The Role of Sleep and Dreaming in Our Emotional Lives.* New York: Oxford University Press.

Cartwright, Rosalind and Lynn Lamberg. 1992. *Crisis Dreaming: Using Your Dreams to Solve Your Problems.* New York: HarperCollins.

Cartwright, Rosalind, S. Lloyd, S. Knight, and I. Trenholme. 1984. "Broken Dreams: A Study of the Effects of Divorce and Depression on Dream Content." *Psychiatry* 47: 251–259.

Catalano, S. 1990. *Children's Dreams in Clinical Practice.* New York: Plenum Press.

Clark, Ronald W. 1980. *Freud: The Man and the Cause.* New York: Random House.

Cole, John. 1992. *The Olympian Dreams and Youthful Rebellion of René Descartes.* Urbana: University of Illinois Press.

Corbin, Henri. 1966. "The Visionary Dream in Islamic Spirituality." In *The Dream and Human Society,* edited by G. E. Von Grunebaum and Roger Callois, 381–408. Berkeley: University of California Press.

Covitz, Joel. 1990. *Visions of the Night: A Study of Jewish Dream Interpretation.* Boston: Shambhala.

Crews, Frederick and Kelly Bulkeley. 2001. "Dialogue with a Skeptic." In *Dreams: A Reader on the Religious, Cultural, and Psychological Dimensions of Dreaming*. New York: Palgrave, 361–377.

Crick, Francis and Graeme Mitchison. 1983. "The Function of Dream Sleep." *Nature* 304: 111–114.

Dang-Vu, Thien Thanh, Manuel Schabus, Martin Desseilles, Sophie Schwartz, and Pierre Maquet. 2007. "Neuroimaging of REM Sleep and Dreaming." In *The New Science of Dreaming*, vol. 1, edited by Deirdre Barrett and Patrick McNamara. Santa Barbara, CA: Praeger.

Dang-Vu, Thien Thanh, et al. 2008. "Spontaneous Neural Activity during Human Slow Wave Sleep." *Proceedings of the National Academy of Sciences* 105: 15160–15165.

Delaney, Gayle. 1979. *Living Your Dreams*. New York: Harper and Row.

Delaney, Gayle. 1991. *Breakthrough Dreaming: How to Tap the Power of Your 24-Hour Mind*. New York: Bantam.

Delaney, Gayle, ed. 1993. *New Directions in Dream Interpretation*. Albany: State University of New York Press.

Dement, William. 1960. "The Effect of Dream Deprivation." *Science* 131: 1705–1707.

Dement, William. 1972. *Some Must Watch While Some Must Sleep: Exploring the World of Sleep*. New York: W.W. Norton.

Dement, William, E. Kahn, and H. Roffwarg. 1965. "The Influence of the Laboratory Situation on the Dreams of the Experimental Subject." *Journal of Nervous and Mental Disease* 149: 119–131.

Dement, William and Nathaniel Kleitman. 1957a. "The Relation of Eye Movements during Sleep to Dream Activity: An Objective Method for the Study of Dreaming." *Journal of Experimental Psychology* 53: 339–346.

Dement, William and Nathaniel Kleitman. 1957b. "Cyclic Variations in EEG during Sleep and Their Relation to Eye Movements, Body Motility, and Dreaming." *Electroencephalography and Clinical Neurophysiology* 9: 673–690.

Dement, William and Christopher Vaughan. 1999. *The Promise of Sleep*. New York: Dell.

Devereux, George, ed. 1951. *Reality and Dream: Psychotherapy of a Plains Indian*. New York: International Universities Press.

Devereux, George. 1953 *Psychoanalysis and the Occult*. New York: International Universities Press.

Devereux, George. 1975. *Dreams in Greek Tragedy: An Ethno-Psychoanalytic Study*. Berkeley: University of California Press.

Domhoff, G. William. 1985. *The Mystique of Dreams: A Search for Utopia through Senoi Dream Theory*. Berkeley: University of California Press.

Domhoff, G. William. 1996. *Finding Meaning in Dreams: A Quantitative Approach*. New York: Plenum.

Domhoff, G. William. 2003. *The Scientific Study of Dreams: Neural Networks, Cognitive Development, and Content Analysis*. Washington, D.C.: American Psychological Association.

Domhoff, G. William. 2011a. "The Neural Substrate for Dreaming: Is It a Subsystem of the Default Network?" *Consciousness and Cognition* 20: 1163–1174.

Domhoff, G. William. 2011b. "Dreams Are Embodied Simulations That Dramatize Conceptions and Concerns: The Continuity Hypothesis in Empirical, Theoretical, and Historical Context." *International Journal of Dream Research* 4: 50–62.

Domhoff, G. William and Adam Schneider. 2008. "Studying Dream Content Using the Archive and Search Engine on DreamBank.net." *Consciousness and Cognition* 17: 1238–1247.

Edwards, Christopher, Perrine Ruby, Josie Malinowski, Paul Bennett, and Mark Blagrove. 2013. "Dreaming and Insight." *Frontiers in Psychology* 24: 979.

Eggan, Dorothy.1952. "The Manifest Content of Dreams: A Challenge to Social Science." *American Anthropologist* 54: 469–485.

Eggan, Dorothy. 1955. "The Personal Use of Myth in Dreams." *Journal of American Folklore* 68: 445–463.

Ekirch, Roger. 2005. *At Day's Close: Night in Times Past*. New York: W.W. Norton.

Ellenberger, Henri. 1970. *The Discovery of the Unconscious: The History and Evolution of Dynamic Psychiatry*. New York: Basic Books.

Erikson, Erik. 1954. "The Dream Specimen of Psychoanalysis." *Journal of the American Psychoanalytical Association* 2: 5–56.

Evans, Christopher. 1983. *Landscapes of the Night: How and Why We Dream* (Peter Evans, ed.). London: V. Gollancz.

Faraday, Ann. 1972. *Dream Power*. New York: Berkley Books.

Faraday, Ann. 1974. *The Dream Game*. New York: Harper and Row.

Feinberg, Irwin. 2004. "Hobson on the Neuroscience of Sleep: A Case of Persistent REM Tunnel Vision." *The American Journal of Psychology* 117: 621–627.

Fosse, Roar, and G. William Domhoff. 2007. "Dreaming as Non-Executive Orienting." In *The New Science of Dreaming*, vol. 2, edited by Patrick McNamara and Deirdre Barrett, 49–78. Santa Barbara, CA: Praeger.

Foulkes, David. 1962. "Dream Reports from Different Stages of Sleep." *The Journal of Abnormal and Social Psychology* 65: 14–25.

Foulkes, David. 1978. *A Grammar of Dreams*. New York: Basic Books.

Foulkes, David. 1982. *Children's Dreams: Longitudinal Studies*. New York: Wiley.

Foulkes, David. 1985. *Dreaming: A Cognitive-Psychological Analysis*. Hillsdale, NJ: Erlbaum.

Foulkes, David. 2002. *Children's Dreaming and the Development of Consciousness*. Cambridge: Harvard University Press.

Fox, Kieran, Savannah Nijeboer, Elizaveta Solomonova, G. William Domhoff, and Kalina Christoff. 2013. "Dreaming as Mind Wandering: Evidence from Functional Neuroimaging and First-Person Content Reports." *Frontiers in Human Neuroscience* 7: 412.

French, Thomas and Erika Fromm. 1964. *Dream Interpretation: A New Approach.* New York: Basic Books.

Freud, Sigmund. 1953–1974. *Standard Edition of the Complete Psychological Works of Sigmund Freud.* Edited by J. Strachey. 24 vols. London: Hogarth Press.

Freud, Sigmund. 1953a. "Dreams and Telepathy." In *Psychoanalysis and the Occult,* edited by G. Devereux. New York: International Universities Press.

Freud, Sigmund. 1953b. "Psychoanalysis and Telepathy." In *Psychoanalysis and the Occult,* edited by G. Devereux. New York: International Universities Press.

Freud, Sigmund. 1953c. "The Occult Significance of Dreams." In *Psychoanalysis and the Occult,* edited by G. Devereux. New York: International Universities Press.

Freud, Sigmund. 1963a. *Dora: Fragment of an Analysis of a Case of Hysteria.* Translated by P. Rieff. New York: Collier Books.

Freud, Sigmund. 1963b. "Remarks upon the Theory and Practice of Dream Interpretation." In *Therapy and Technique,* edited by P. Rieff, 205–218. New York: Collier Books.

Freud, Sigmund. 1963c. "Some Additional Notes on Dream Interpretation as a Whole." In *Therapy and Technique,* edited by P. Rieff, 219–232. New York: Collier Books.

Freud, Sigmund. 1965a. *The Interpretation of Dreams.* Translated by James Strachey. New York: Avon Books.

Freud, Sigmund. 1965b. *New Introductory Lectures on Psychoanalysis.* Translated by J. Strachey. New York: W.W. Norton.

Freud, Sigmund. 1966. *Introductory Lectures on Psychoanalysis.* Translated by J. Strachey. New York: W.W. Norton.

Freud, Sigmund. 1980. *On Dreams.* Translated by J. Strachey. New York: W.W. Norton.

Gackenbach, Jayne, ed. 1987. *Sleep and Dreams: A Source Book.* New York: Garland.

Gackenbach, Jayne. 1991. "Frameworks for Understanding Lucid Dreaming: A Review." *Dreaming* 1: 109–128.

Gackenbach, Jayne. 2006. "Video Game Play and Lucid Dreams: Implications for the Development of Consciousness." *Dreaming* 16: 96–110.

Gackenbach, Jayne and J. Bosveld. 1989. *Control Your Dreams.* New York: Harper and Row.

Gackenbach, Jayne, and Stephen LaBerge, eds. 1988. *Conscious Mind, Sleeping Brain: Perspectives on Lucid Dreaming.* New York: Plenum.

Garfield, Patricia. 1974. *Creative Dreaming.* New York: Ballantine.

Garfield, Patricia. 1989. *Pathway to Ecstasy: The Way of the Dream Mandala.* Englewood Cliffs: Prentice Hall.

Garfield, Patricia. 1991. *The Healing Power of Dreams.* New York: Fireside Books.

Gay, Peter. 1988. *Freud: A Life for Our Time*. New York: W.W. Norton.

Germain, Anne, Tore Nielsen, Antonio Zadra, and Jacques Montplaisir. 2003. "The Prevalence of Typical Dream Themes Challenges the Specificity of the Threat Simulation Theory." In *Sleep and Dreaming: Scientific Advances and Reconsiderations*, edited by Edward Pace-Schott, Mark Solms, Mark Blagrove, and Stevan Harnad, 151–152. Cambridge: Cambridge University Press.

Glaskin, Katie and Richard Chenhall. 2013. *Sleep Around the World: Anthropological Perspectives*. New York: Palgrave Macmillan.

Green, Celia. 1968. *Lucid Dreams*. Oxford: Institute of Psychophysical Research.

Greenberg, R., R. Pillard, and C. Pearlman. 1972. "The Effect of Dream (REM) Deprivation on Adaptation to Stress." *Psychosomatic Medicine* 34: 257–262.

Griffith, Richard, Otoya Miyagi, and Akira Tago. 1958. "The Universality of Typical Dreams: Japanese vs. Americans." *American Anthropologist* 60: 1173–1179.

Hall, Calvin. 1966. *The Meaning of Dreams*. New York: McGraw-Hill.

Hall, Calvin. 1967. "Representation of the Laboratory Setting in Dreams." *Journal of Nervous and Mental Disease* 144: 198–206.

Hall, Calvin and G. William Domhoff. 1963. "A Ubiquitous Sex Difference in Dreams." *Journal of Abnormal and Social Psychology* 66: 278–280.

Hall, Calvin and R. Lind. 1970. *Dreams, Life, and Literature: A Study of Franz Kafka*. Chapel Hill: University of North Carolina Press.

Hall, Calvin and Vernon Nordby. 1972. *The Individual and His Dreams*. New York: Signet.

Hall, Calvin and Robert Van de Castle. 1966. *The Content Analysis of Dreams*. New York: Appleton-Century-Crofts.

Hartmann, Ernest. 1967. *The Biology of Dreaming*. Springfield: Charles C. Thomas.

Hartmann, Ernest. 1973. *The Functions of Sleep*. New Haven: Yale University Press.

Hartmann, Ernest. 1984. *The Nightmare: The Psychology and Biology of Terrifying Dreams*. New York: Basic Books.

Hartmann, Ernest. 1991. *Boundaries of the Mind: A New Psychology of Personality*. New York: Basic Books.

Hartmann, Ernest. 2000. *Dreams and Nightmares: The Origin and Meaning of Dreams*. New York: Basic Books.

Hermansen, Marcia. 2001. "Dreams and Dreaming in Islam." In *Dreams: A Reader on the Religious, Cultural, and Psychological Dimensions of Dreaming*, edited by Kelly Bulkeley, 73–92. New York: Palgrave.

Hillman, James. 1979. *The Dream and the Underworld*. New York: Harper and Row.

Hobson, J. Allan. 1988. *The Dreaming Brain*. New York: Basic Books, 1988.

Hobson, J. Allan. 2003. *Dreaming: An Introduction to the Science of Sleep*. New York: Oxford University Press.

Hobson, J. Allan. 1988. *The Dreaming Brain: How the Brain Creates Both the Sense and the Nonsense of Dreams*. New York: Basic Books.

Hobson, J. Allan. 1999. *Dreaming as Delirium: How the Brain Goes out of Its Mind*. Cambridge, MA: MIT Press.

Hobson, J. Allan, S. A. Hoffman, R. Helfand, and D. Kostner. 1987. "Dream Bizarreness and the Activation-Synthesis Hypothesis." *Human Neurobiology* 6: 157–164.

Hobson, J. Allan and Robert McCarley. 1977. "The Brain as a Dream-State Generator: An Activation-Synthesis Hypothesis of the Dream Process." *American Journal of Psychiatry* 134: 1335–1368.

Homans, Peter. 1989. *The Ability to Mourn: Disillusionment and the Social Origins of Psychoanalysis*. Chicago: University of Chicago Press.

Horne, Jim. 2007. *Sleepfaring: A Journey through the Science of Sleep*. New York: Oxford University Press.

Hufford, David. 1982. *The Terror That Comes in the Night: An Experience-Centered Study of Supernatural Assault Traditions*. Philadelphia: University of Pennsylvania Press.

Hunt, Harry. 1989. *The Multiplicity of Dreams: Memory, Imagination, and Consciousness*. New Haven: Yale University Press.

Hunt, Harry. 2003. "New Multiplicities of Dreaming and REMing." In *Sleep and Dreaming: Scientific Advances and Reconsiderations*, edited by Edward Pace-Schott, Mark Solms, Mark Blagrove, and Stevan Harnad, 164–166. New York: Cambridge University Press.

Hurd, Ryan. 2010. *Sleep Paralysis: A Guide to Hypnagogic Visions and Visitors of the Night*. Los Altos: Hyena Press.

Hurd, Ryan. 2014. "Unearthing the Paleolithic Mind in Lucid Dreams." In *Lucid Dreaming: New Perspectives on Consciousness in Sleep*, edited by Ryan Hurd and Kelly Bulkeley, 277–324. Santa Barbara, CA: ABC-CLIO.

Hurd, Ryan and Kelly Bulkeley, eds. 2014. *Lucid Dreaming: New Perspectives on Consciousness in Sleep*. Santa Barbara, CA: ABC-CLIO.

Irwin, Lee. 1994. *The Dream Seekers: Native American Visionary Traditions of the Great Plains*. Norman, OK: University of Oklahoma Press.

Jedrej, M.C., and Rosalind Shaw, eds. 1992. *Dreaming, Religion, and Society in Africa*. Leiden: E.J. Brill.

Jones, Ernest. 1951. *On the Nightmare*. New York: Liveright, 1951.

Jouvet, Michel. 1999. *The Paradox of Sleep: The Story of Dreaming*. Translated by Laurence Garey. Cambridge, MA: MIT Press.

Jung, Carl. 1965. *Memories, Dreams, Reflections*. Translated by R. and C. Winston. New York: Vintage.

Jung, Carl. 1967. *The Collected Works of C.G. Jung*. Translated by R. Hull. Twenty volumes. Princeton: Princeton University Press.

Jung, Carl. 1974. *Dreams*. Translated by R. Hull. Princeton: Princeton University Press.

Jung, Carl. 2008. *Children's Dreams: Notes from the Seminar Given in 1936–1940.* Translated by Ernst Falzeder and Tony Woolfson. Princeton: Princeton University Press.

Kahan, Tracey. 2001. "Consciousness in Dreaming: A Metacognitive Approach." In *Dreams: A Reader on the Religious, Cultural, and Psychological Dimensions of Dreaming,* edited by Kelly Bulkeley, 333–360. New York: Palgrave.

Kahan, Tracey. 2003. "The 'Problem' of Dreaming in NREM Sleep Continues to Challenge Reductionist (Two Generator) Models of Dream Generation." In *Sleep and Dreaming: Scientific Advances and Reconsiderations,* edited by Edward Pace-Schott, Mark Solms, Mark Blagrove, and Stevan Harnad, 167–169. Cambridge: Cambridge University Press.

Kahan, Tracey and Stephen LaBerge. 2011. "Dreaming and Waking: Similarities and Differences Revisited." *Consciousness and Cognition* 20: 494–515.

Knudson, Roger. 2001. "Significant Dreams: Bizarre or Beautiful?" *Dreaming* 11: 166–177.

Knudson, Roger and Samuel Minier. 1999. "The On-Going Significance of Significant Dreams: The Case of the Bodiless Head." *Dreaming* 9: 235–245.

Kracke, Waud. 2001. "Kagwahiv Mourning: Dreams of a Bereaved Father." In *Dreams: A Reader on the Religious, Cultural, and Psychological Dimensions of Dreaming,* edited by Kelly Bulkeley, 175–188. New York: Palgrave.

Kramer, Milton. 1991. "The Nightmare: A Failure in Dream Function." Dreaming 1: 277–286.

Kramer, Milton, ed. 2015 *Dream Research: Contributions to Clinical Practice.* New York: Routledge.

Krippner, Stanley, Fariba Bogzaran, and Andre Percia de Carvalho. 2002. *Extraordinary Dreams and How to Work with Them.* Albany: State University of New York Press.

Kryger, Meir H., Thomas Roth, and William C. Dement. 2005. *Principles and Practice of Sleep Medicine.* Fourth Edition. Philadelphia: Elsevier Saunders.

Kuiken, Don. 1995. "Dreams and Feeling Realization." *Dreaming* 5: 129–158.

Kuiken, Don and L. Smith. 1991. "Impactful Dreams and Metaphor Generation." *Dreaming* 1: 135–146.

Kuiken, Don and Shelley Sikora. 1993. "The Impact of Dreams on Waking Thoughts and Feelings." In *The Functions of Dreaming,* edited by Alan Moffitt, Milton Kramer, and Robert Hoffmann, 419–476. Albany: State University of New York Press.

LaBerge, Stephen. 1985. *Lucid Dreaming.* Los Angeles: Jeremy Tarcher.

Lakoff, George. 2001. "How Metaphor Structures Dreams: The Theory of Conceptual Metaphor Applied to Dream Analysis." In *Dreams: A Reader on the Religious, Cultural, and Psychological Dimensions of Dreaming,* edited by Kelly Bulkeley, 265–284. New York: Palgrave.

Lavie, Peretz and Hanna Kaminer. 1991. "Dreams That Poison Sleep: Dreams in Holocaust Survivors." *Dreaming* 1: 11–22.

Leslie, Kenneth and Robert Ogilvie. 1996. "Vestibular Dreams: The Effect of Rocking on Dream Mentation." *Dreaming* 6: 1–16.

Lohmann, Roger, ed. 2003. *Dream Travelers: Sleep Experiences and Culture in the Western Pacific*. New York: Palgrave Macmillan.

Lortie-Lussier, Monique, S. Simond, N. Rinfret, and J. DeKoninck. 1987. "Working Mothers versus Homemakers: Do Dreams Reflect the Changing Roles of Women?" *Sex Roles* 12: 1009–1021.

Lortie-Lussier, Monique, S. Simond, N. Rinfret, and J. DeKoninck. 1992. "Beyond Sex Differences: Family and Occupational Roles' Impact on Women's and Men's Dreams." *Sex Roles* 26: 79–96.

Malcolm, Norman. 1959. *Dreaming*. London: Routledge and Kegan Paul.

Maquet, Pierre, Carlyle Smith, and Robert Stickgold, eds. 2003. *Sleep and Brain Plasticity*. New York: Oxford University Press.

Masson, Jeffrey M., ed. 1985. *The Complete Letters of Sigmund Freud to Wilhelm Fliess, 1887-1904*. Cambridge: Belknap.

McGuire, W., ed. 1974. *The Freud/Jung Letters: The Correspondence between Sigmund Freud and C.G. Jung*. Princeton: Princeton University Press.

McNamara, Patrick. 2004. *An Evolutionary Psychology of Sleep and Dreams*. Westport, CT: Praeger.

McNamara, Patrick, Robert Barton, and Charles Nunn, eds. 2010. *Evolution of Sleep: Phylogenetic and Functional Perspectives*. New York: Cambridge University Press.

McNamara, Patrick and Kelly Bulkeley. 2015. "Dreams as a Source of Supernatural Agent Concepts." *Frontiers in Psychology* 6: 283.

Mittermaier, Amira. 2010. *Dreams That Matter: Egyptian Landscapes of the Imagination*. Berkeley: University of California Press.

Moffitt, Alan, Milton Kramer, and Robert Hoffmann, eds. 1993. *The Functions of Dreaming*. Albany: State University of New York Press.

Nielsen, Tore. 2003. "A Review of Mentation in REM and NREM Sleep: 'Covert' REM Sleep as a Possible Reconciliation of Two Opposing Models." In *Sleep and Dreaming: Scientific Advances and Reconsiderations*, edited by Edward Pace-Schott, Mark Solms, Mark Blagrove, and Stevan Harnad, 59–74. Cambridge University Press.

Nielsen, Tore and Ross Levin, 2007. "Nightmares: A New Neurocognitive Model." *Sleep Medicine Reviews* 11: 295–310.

Nofzinger, E. A., M. A. Mintun, M. B. Wiseman, D. J. Kupfer, and R. Y. Moore. 1997. "Forebrain Activation in REM Sleep: An FDG PET Study." *Brain Research* 770: 192–201.

O'Flaherty, Wendy Doniger. 1984. *Dreams, Illusion, and Other Realities*. Chicago: University of Chicago Press.

Olsen, Chris. 2014. "Forgotten Perspectives on Lucid Dreaming from the Enlightenment through the Early Twentieth Century." In *Lucid Dreaming: New Perspectives on Consciousness in Sleep*, vol. 2, edited by Ryan Hurd and Kelly Bulkeley, 93–125. Santa Barbara, CA: ABC-CLIO.

Pace-Schott, Edward, Mark Solms, Mark Blagrove, and Stevan Harnad, eds. *Sleep and Dreaming: Scientific Advances and Reconsiderations*. Cambridge University Press, 2003.

Pagel, James. 2010. *The Limits of Dream: A Scientific Exploration of the Mind/Brain Interface*. New York: Academic Press.

Pagel, James. 2014. "Lucid Dreaming as Sleep Meditation." In *Lucid Dreaming: New Perspectives on Consciousness in Sleep*, vol. 1, edited by Ryan Hurd and Kelly Bulkeley, 63–76. Santa Barbara, CA: ABC-CLIO.

Panksepp, Jaak. 2003. "'The Dream of Reason Creates Monsters' . . . Especially When We Neglect the Role of Emotions in REM-States." In *Sleep and Dreaming: Scientific Advances and Reconsiderations*, edited by Edward Pace-Schott, Mark Solms, Mark Blagrove, and Stevan Harnad, 200–202. Cambridge: Cambridge University Press.

Patton, Kimberley. 2004. "'A Great and Strange Correction': Intentionality, Locality, and Epiphany in the Category of Dream Incubation." *History of Religions* 43: 194–223.

Perls, Frederick. 1970a. "Dream Seminars." In *Gestalt Therapy Now*, edited by J. F. Shepherd and I. L. Shepherd, 204–233. New York: Harper Colophon.

Perls, Frederick. 1970b. "Four Lectures." In *Gestalt Therapy Now*, edited by J. F. Shepherd and I. L. Shepherd, 14–38. New York: Harper Colophon.

Piaget, Jean. 1962. *Play, Dreams, and Imitation in Childhood*. Translated by C. Gattegno and F. M. Hodgson. New York: W.W. Norton.

Purcell, Sheila, Alan Moffitt, and Robert Hoffmann. 1993. "Waking, Dreaming, and Self-Regulation." In *The Functions of Dreaming*, edited by Alan Moffitt, Milton Kramer, and Robert Hoffmann, 197–260. Albany: State University of New York Press.

Rahman, Fazlur. 1966. "Dream, Imagination, and *Alam al-mithal*." In *The Dream and Human Society*, edited by G. E. Von Grunebaum and Roger Callois, 409–420. Berkeley: University of California Press.

Raichle, Marcus and Abraham Snyder. 2007. "A Default Mode of Brain Function: A Brief History of an Evolving Idea." *NeuroImage* 37: 1083–1090.

Rasch, Bjorn and Jan Born. 2013. "About Sleep's Role in Memory." *Physiological Reviews* 93: 681–766.

Rechtschaffen, Alan. 1978. "The Single-Mindedness and Isolation of Dreams." *Sleep* 1: 97–109.

Revonsuo, Antii. 2003. "The Reinterpretation of Dreams: An Evolutionary Hypothesis of the Function of Dreaming." In *Sleep and Dreaming: Scientific Advances and Reconsiderations*, edited by Edward Pace-Schott, Mark Solms, Mark Blagrove, and Stevan Harnad, 85–109. Cambridge: Cambridge University Press.

Revonsuo, Antti and Christina Salmivalli. 1995. "A Content Analysis of Bizarre Elements in Dreams." *Dreaming* 5: 169–188.

Roffwarg, Howard, Joseph Muzio, and William Dement. 1966. "Ontogenetic Development of the Human Sleep-Dream Cycle." *Science* 152: 604–619.

Sandman, N., K. Valli, E. Kronholm, H. M. Ollila, A. Revonsuo, T. Laatikainen, and T. Paunio. 2013. "Nightmares: Prevalence among the Finnish General Adult Population and War Veterans during 1972–2007." *Sleep* 36: 1041–1050.

Schredl, Michael. 2007. "Dream Recall: Models and Empirical Data." In *The New Science of Dreaming*, vol 2, edited by Patrick McNamara and Deirdre Barrett, 79–114. Santa Barbara, CA: Praeger.

Schredl, Michael, Petra Ciric, Simon Gotz, and Lutz Wittmann. 2004. "Typical Dreams: Stability and Gender Differences." *The Journal of Psychology* 138: 485–494.

Shafton, Anthony. 1995. *Dream Reader: Contemporary Approaches to the Understanding of Dreams*. Albany: State University of New York Press.

Shweder, Richard, Lene Arnett Jensen, and William Goldstein. 1995. "Who Sleeps by Whom Revisited: A Method for Extracting the Moral Goods Implicit in Practice." *New Directions for Child and Adolescent Development* 67: 21–29.

Siegel, Alan. 1990. *Dreams That Can Change Your Life*. Los Angeles: Jeremy Tarcher.

Snyder, Frederick, Ismet Karacan, K. Van Tharp, Jr., and Jimmy Scott. 1968. "Phenomenology of REM Sleep Dreaming." *Psychophysiology* 4: 375.

Smith, Carlyle. 1993. "REM Sleep and Learning: Some Recent Findings." In *The Functions of Dreaming*, edited by Alan Moffitt, Milton Kramer, and Robert Hoffmann. Albany: State University of New York Press.

Solms, Mark. 1997. *The Neuropsychology of Dreams: A Clinico-Anatomical Study*. Mahwah, NJ: Lawrence Erlbaum.

Stepansky, R., B. Holzinger, A. Schmeiser-Rieder, B. Saletu, M. Kunze, and J. Zeitlhofer. 1998. "Austrian Dream Behavior: Results of a Representative Population Survey." *Dreaming* 8: 23–30.

Stewart, Kilton. 1969. "Dream Theory in Malaya." In *Altered States of Consciousness*, edited by Charles Tart, 191–204. New York: Harper Collins.

Stumbrys, Tadas and Daniel Erlacher. 2014. "The Science of Lucid Dream Induction." In *Lucid Dreaming: New Perspectives on Consciousness in Sleep*, vol. 1, edited by Ryan Hurd and Kelly Bulkeley, 77–102. Santa Barbara, CA: ABC-CLIO.

Sumegi, Angela. 2008. *Dreamworlds of Shamanism and Tibetan Buddhism: The Third Place*. Albany: State University of New York Press.

Szpakowska, Kasia. 2001. "Through the Looking Glass: Dreams in Ancient Egypt." In *Dreams: A Reader on the Religious, Cultural, and Psychological Dimensions of Dreaming*, edited by Kelly Bulkeley, 29–44. New York: Palgrave.

Taylor, Jeremy. 1983. *Dream Work: Techniques for Discovering the Creative Power in Dreams*. Mahwah, NJ: Paulist Press.

Taylor, Jeremy. 1992. *Where People Fly and Water Runs Uphill: Using Dreams to Tap the Wisdom of the Unconscious*. New York: Warner Books.

Taylor, Jeremy. 1995. "Debate on the Legacy of the Senoi." *Association for the Study of Dreams Newsletter* 12, no. 2: 30–34.

Tedlock, Barbara. 2005. *The Woman in the Shaman's Body: Reclaiming the Feminine in Religion and Medicine.* New York: Bantam.

Ullman, Montague and Nan Zimmerman. 1979. *Working with Dreams.* Los Angeles: Jeremy Tarcher.

Van de Castle, Robert. 1994. *Our Dreaming Mind.* New York: Ballantine Books.

Vertes, Robert and Kathleen Eastman. 2003. "The Case against Memory Consolidation in REM Sleep." In *Sleep and Dreaming: Scientific Advances and Reconsiderations*, edited by Edward Pace-Schott, Mark Solms, Mark Blagrove, and Stevan Harnad, 75–84. Cambridge: Cambridge University Press.

Wamsley, Erin, Yasutaka Hirota, Matthew Tucker, Mark Smith, and John Antrobus. 2007. "Circadian and Ultradian Influences on Dreaming: A Dual Rhythm Model." *Brain Research Bulletin* 71: 347–354.

Winget, Carolyn and Milton Kramer. 1978. *Dimensions of Dreams.* Gainesville: University of Florida Press.

Wolman, Richard and Miloslava Kozmova. 2007. "'Last Night I Had the Strangest Dream': Varieties of Rational Thought Processes in Dream Reports." *Consciousness and Cognition* 16: 838–849.

Young, Serinity. 2001. "Buddhist Dream Experience: The Role of Interpretation, Ritual, and Gender." In *Dreams: A Reader on the Religious, Cultural, and Psychological Dimensions of Dreaming*, edited by Kelly Bulkeley, 9–28. New York: Palgrave.

Yu, Calvin. 2010. "Dream Intensity Scale: Factors in the Phenomenological Analysis of Dreams." *Dreaming* 20: 107–129.

Index

Accommodation, 80–81, 99
Activation-synthesis hypothesis, 67–70, 91
Active imagination, 35
Adler, Alfred, 44–46, 47, 56–57, 123, 130–131
AIM model, 70–71
Amplification, 34, 41, 43, 47, 57, 130
Anima, 37, 40
Animus, 37, 40
Aquinas, Thomas, 8
Archetypes, 35–38, 39, 90, 122
Aristotle, 5, 7–9, 12, 110, 131–132
Artemidorus, 5, 10–13, 18, 101, 132
Aserinsky, Eugene, 61–62, 65, 67, 125
Assimilation, 80–81, 99

Basel, Switzerland, 30
Beck, Aaron, 54
Belicki, Kathryn, 97–99
Beradt, Charlotte, 43
Bible, 5–7, 12, 18, 67, 131
Big dreams, 39
Binswanger, Ludwig, 46
Bollacker, Kurt, 134
Boss, Medard, 44, 46–49, 56–57, 123–124, 130–131
Boundaries of the mind, 94, 95–96, 99, 128
Brock University, 90

Cartwright, Rosalind, 64–65
Children's dreams, 19, 30, 76, 79, 80–82, 88, 95, 99, 102, 112
Cincinnati, Ohio, 75
Clark University, 36
Cognitive Behavioral Therapy (CBT), 54
Cognitive-Experiential approach, 44, 54–56, 125
Collective unconscious, 36, 81–82
Community, 7, 11, 102, 107, 110, 114, 131
Compensation, 32, 40, 43, 122
Condensation, 21, 27, 68
Consciousness, 4, 23–24, 27, 30, 32–33, 35, 37, 45, 47, 89, 91, 102, 104, 111, 114, 116, 130
Considerations of representability, 22, 27
Content analysis, 82–86, 126–127, 139
Continuity hypothesis, 85, 135, 141
Crick, Francis, 73–74, 126, 130

Default network, 86
Delaney, Gayle, 105–106, 107, 111, 116, 128, 131
Dement, William, 61, 63, 66, 76, 125
Discontinuity hypothesis, 135, 140–141

Displacement, 22, 27

Domhoff, G. William, 86–87, 113–114, 126–127, 130, 133–134, 139

DreamBank, 86–87, 133–134

Dream incubation, 98, 103, 105, 106, 116, 117, 128–129

"Dream of Irma's Injection," 15, 18–20, 21, 121

Dream sharing groups, 107–110, 117, 131

Dreams-within-dreams (lucid dreams), 23, 49, 70–71, 90, 104–105, 110–111, 116, 117, 129

EEG (Electroencephalograph), 65, 70, 75, 110, 111, 125

Ego Psychology, 44, 49–51, 124

Ellis, Albert, 54

Emotions, 2, 8, 45, 50, 57, 66, 83, 97, 122

Erikson, Erik, 49

Esalen Institute, 51, 113

Evolution, 4, 36, 38, 63, 78, 80

Existential Psychoanalysis, 44, 46–49, 124–125

Faraday, Ann, 102–104, 107, 111, 114, 116, 128, 131

Fliess, Wilhelm, 16, 17

Formation of dreams, 4, 12, 24, 27, 40, 56, 67, 71–72, 77, 89, 91–92, 99, 116, 129–132

Foulkes, David, 66–67, 76–77, 87–89, 90, 91–92, 93, 99–100, 127, 129, 130

Free association, 18, 28, 34, 43, 45, 49, 57, 84, 130

French, Thomas and Fromm, Erika, 44, 49–51, 56–57, 124, 130–131

Freud, Anna, 49

Freud, Sigmund, 3, 15–28, 29, 31, 32, 34, 36, 43–44, 45, 46, 47, 49, 51, 54, 56, 57, 59–60, 67, 70, 71, 80, 81–82, 84, 89, 91–92, 97, 102, 103, 110, 120, 121–2, 126, 129, 131–132

Function of dreams, 4, 12, 27, 32–33, 45–46, 56–57, 71, 77–78, 89, 99, 116–117, 131–132

Garfield, Patricia, 104–105, 107, 111, 113, 114, 116, 128, 131

Gestalt psychology, 44, 51–53, 103, 124–125

Green, Celia, 110

Hall, Calvin, 75, 82–86, 99–100, 126–127, 129, 130–132, 139

Hartmann, Ernest, 75–76, 93–97, 99, 128, 130

Hartmann, Heinz, 49

Hearne, Keith, 110

Heidegger, Martin, 46

Hill, Clara, 44, 54–56, 57, 125, 131

Hillman, James, 91–92

Hobson, J. Allan, 65, 67–71, 78, 91–92, 125–126, 129, 130

Hunt, Harry, 90–93, 99–100, 127–128, 130, 131, 135

Individual Psychology, 44

Individuation, 38

Inferiority versus superiority, 44–45

International Association for the Study of Dreams (IASD), 101, 115

Interpretation of dreams, 5, 7, 9, 10–13, 18–19, 27–28, 33–34, 35, 41, 43, 45, 47, 50–51, 54–56, 57, 69, 72, 74, 78, 84, 85, 100, 103, 106, 109, 112, 117, 119, 121–129, 130–132

Isomorphism, 65–66, 68, 78

Jouvet, Michel, 63

Jung, Carl, 3, 29–41, 43–44, 45, 46, 47, 54, 56, 57, 70, 81–82, 84, 91–92, 97, 102, 103, 105, 120, 122–123, 129, 131–132, 135

Kleitman, Nathaniel, 61–62, 65, 67, 125

Kramer, Milton, 55

"Lab effect," 74–77
LaBerge, Stephen, 110–111, 116, 128, 130
Language, 4
Latent content versus manifest content, 19, 21–23, 26, 32, 47, 70, 84
Learning, 64, 77
London, 16
Lucid dreams. *See* Dreams-within-dreams

Maimonides Medical Center, 107
Mandalas, 38
Manifest content versus latent content, 19, 21–23, 26, 32, 47, 70, 84
McCarley, Robert, 67–68
Memory, 2, 4, 5, 8, 22, 54, 79, 89, 96, 97–99
Mitchison, Graeme, 73–74, 126, 130

Nightmares, 6, 19–20, 37, 53, 54, 71, 75–76, 81, 86, 90, 94–96, 127, 128, 138
Night terrors, 94–95
Nocturnal emissions, 75
Nordby, Vernon, 82
NREM sleep, 59–74, 77–78, 87, 94

Objective and subjective levels, 34–35, 41, 52
Oedipus complex, 19, 121

Perls, Frederick, 44, 51–53, 56–57, 124–125, 130–131
Persona, 37, 40, 122
Personal unconscious, 36
Physical influences on dreams, 3, 90
Piaget, Jean, 80–82, 99, 130
Plato, 7–8
Post-traumatic nightmares, 25, 95
Preconscious, 23–24
Preminger, Otto, 105–106
Primary process, 24

Prophecy, 6, 8–9, 10–11, 33, 48, 67, 90, 93, 127
Projection, 53, 84, 109–110, 129
Prospective function, 33, 40–41
Psychoanalysis, 31, 32, 44, 46, 49, 51, 67, 70, 107
Psychotherapy, 3, 28, 30, 33, 35, 39, 44, 45, 47–48, 49, 51, 52, 54–56, 60, 84, 101, 111, 131

Reason, 2
Rebound effect, 64
Religion, 3, 5–7, 9, 11, 12, 30, 31, 34, 36, 38, 39, 48, 49, 53, 55, 57, 87, 90, 91, 116, 131
REM sleep, 3, 54, 59–74, 77–78, 80, 87, 91, 94, 97, 102, 125–126, 130
Repetition dimension, 86
Reverse learning, 73–74

Salk Institute, 73
Sears, Robert, 134
Secondary process, 24
Secondary revision, 23, 27
Self, 37, 38, 40
Senoi, 111–115
Sexuality, 19–20, 22, 31, 48, 75–76
Shadow, 37, 40, 43
Shafton, Anthony, 46
Skepticism, 7, 8–9, 10, 111
Sleep, 4, 5, 8, 12, 18, 24, 61–63, 68–69, 111
Sleep and Dream Database, 86–87, 116, 133–141
Sleep deprivation, 63–64
Sleep laboratory, 3, 60–65, 74–77, 80, 87, 90, 94, 97, 101, 102, 110–111, 116, 125, 129
Solms, Mark, 71–73, 78, 126
Spangler, Patricia, 55
Stanford University, 110–111
Stewart, Kilton, 111–115
Subjective and objective levels, 34–35, 41, 52
Sublimation, 25

Superiority versus inferiority, 44–45
Symbols, 9, 11, 18, 22–23, 27, 28, 30,
    32, 34, 35–38, 39, 40–41, 47, 68,
    81–82, 84, 86, 91, 103, 121–129,
    130

Taylor, Jeremy, 107–8, 111, 114, 116,
    128–129, 131
Telepathy, 25, 26
Theory of mind, 73
Topdog versus underdog, 53–54, 103,
    124–125
Tufts University, 93

Ullman, Montague, 107–108, 128, 131
Unconscious, 19, 23–24, 25, 27,
    30–33, 35, 37–39, 40, 43, 45, 47,
    70, 81–82, 84, 91, 121–123, 129

Underdog versus topdog, 53–54, 103,
    124–125
University of Chicago, 3, 61, 67, 87
University of Maryland, 54
University of Wyoming, 88

Van de Castle, Robert, 75, 82–86,
    129, 139
Vienna, 16, 44

Walsh, Mary, 134
Western society, 5, 38–39, 41, 115
Whitman, R., 75
Wish-fulfillment, 19–20, 23, 26,
    121, 126

Zimmerman, Nan, 107
Zurich, 40, 46

About the Author

Kelly Bulkeley, PhD, is a psychologist of religion focusing on dreams and dreaming. He is director of the Sleep and Dream Database (SDDb), a senior editor of the APA journal *Dreaming*, and a former president of the International Association for the Study of Dreams. He is author and editor of several books, including *The Wilderness of Dreams* (SUNY Press, 1994), *The Wondering Brain* (Routledge, 2005), *American Dreamers* (Beacon, 2008), *Dreaming in the World's Religions* (New York University Press, 2008), *Lucid Dreaming* (with Ryan Hurd, ABC-CLIO, 2014), and *Big Dreams: The Science of Dreaming and the Origins of Religion* (Oxford University Press, 2016).